UNLOCKING THE POWER OF YOUR P!

PRAYER | PURPOSE | PASSION | PAST | PAUSE | PRESENCE | PARTNERSHIP | POTENTIAL | PRESENTATION | PAIN | PERSISTENCE | PEN

LAKESHA WOMACK

© 2019 LaKesha Womack

All rights reserved. No part of this book may be reproduced or transmitted in any form or by any means, electronic or mechanical, including photocopying, recording, or by any information storage or retrieval system, without permission in writing from the publisher.

ISBN: 9781795641807

INTRODUCTION

So often we maneuver through life feeling powerless. We forget how much control we actually have over our lives. Of course, we cannot control other people and there are circumstances that no matter how hard we try, they are beyond our control. However, there is a lot in our lives that we do have control over. There are many areas that seem hopeless but with the right frame of mind, we can discover our greatest strengths.

Unlocking the Power of Your P! will guide you through twelve areas of your life that are sources of personal power that can lead to professional growth. You may find that you have already mastered some of these areas while others are a work in progress. It is important to note that life is a work in progress. We should always strive to find areas for growth and development. Even if you think you are doing well in an area, read through the content and see if there are ways that you can improve.

Guess what?!? I want to grow also! That may sound strange coming from the person writing the book but if you read through the strategies of each section and have some ideas of how I can improve, share it on my social media and tag me with **#PowerOfP**. I hope you believe that we are doing this thing called life together. You are not an island, and neither am I. We are a team and teamwork makes the dream work so share some strategies that have worked to help you unlock your power in the different areas that we are discussing.

Once you have read the section and answered the questions, there will be a declaration page. On this page, you should write a statement of affirmation – **I will unlock my power by…** In this space, take your power and verbalize it! Make a bold statement about yourself and for yourself. You may need to refer back to this statement if you begin to feel stuck or forget why you are doing the work in this area of your life.

Finally, at the end of each section, I want you to start setting goals so that you can begin to experience the changes that you seek in your life. Based on your statement of affirmation, you should set:

- **Long Term Goals/Your Vision** – this is where you should dare to dream! Look ahead to the future and imagine where you want to be in life. What does that look like? Based on your affirmation, write a few sentences to describe what this reimagined life will look like and don't be afraid to change. You are not a tree. You can always switch directions if you find that a goal no longer serves you, is not what you are passionate about, or that you don't have the resources to implement.

- **Short Term Goals** – what you can begin to work on with a goal of completing within the next year? Think big but also think realistically. Knowing your human and financial resources, what S.M.A.R.T. (**S**pecific, **M**easurable, **A**ttainable, **R**ealistic, and **T**imely) goals can you set for yourself? Since there are twelve areas that you are potentially working on, I would not advise setting more than one goal for each section. Think about what goal is needed to achieve the long-term vision. Once you complete the goal, you can always add others. Also, do not be alarmed if your goals begin to overlap with other areas. That is actually a good thing and will help to see how the different areas of your life are aligned.

- **Immediate Goals** – what can you do right now to implement change in your life? When you look at the short-term goal and begin to break down the steps, what can you get started on right now? In some cases, it may be a change in mindset or even a change in a daily behavior.

You will notice that we are working backward instead of starting with the immediate action items. To truly unlock the power that will lead to your success, you have to visualize what a successful life will look like and then begin putting action items in place to make it a reality. Change does not happen overnight, and you will not become successful simply by dreaming. You must also plan and do.

The most important piece of advice that I can provide is to work at your own pace. Do not feel pressured by family, friends, society, coworkers, social media, or anyone else to achieve your goals on THEIR timeline. Be mindful of where you are headed and enjoy the journey because there are life lessons to be learned along the path that often get missed because we are so focused on the destination.

I hope you are ready to discover some techniques to unlock the power of your life. We only get one shot at living our best life and it is my goal to help you do that.

Let's get started!

Contents

UNLOCKING THE POWER OF PRAYER _____ 10

UNLOCKING THE POWER OF PURPOSE _____ 29

UNLOCKING THE POWER OF PASSION _____ 44

UNLOCKING THE POWER OF YOUR PAST _____ 62

UNLOCKING THE POWER OF THE PAUSE _____ 84

UNLOCKING THE POWER OF YOUR PRESENCE ___ 101

UNLOCKING THE POWER OF PARTNERSHIP _____ 121

UNLOCKING THE POWER OF YOUR POTENTIAL ___ 146

UNLOCKING THE POWER OF YOUR PRESENTATION 163

UNLOCKING THE POWER OF PAIN _____ 179

UNLOCKING THE POWER OF PERSISTENCE _____ 197

UNLOCKING THE POWER OF YOUR PEN _____ 211

ABOUT THE AUTHOR – LAKESHA WOMACK _____ 227

"Nearly all men can stand adversity, but if you want to test a man's character, give him power."

— Abraham Lincoln

UNLOCKING THE POWER OF PRAYER

A few years ago, I decided to rebrand Womack Consulting Group, the company that I established in 2005. As I was thinking about the identity of my brand, I was reminded of the advice that I am sure some of you have received – don't mix business with religion or politics. I contemplated this advice for many months as I was considering my new brand identity.

Could I do what I do without the power of prayer?

Could I work effectively with my clients without praying for them and praying with them?

Could I be a leader without the help of God?

For some of you the answer may be, "yes" but for me, the answer was "absolutely not!"

I pray before each presentation. I pray over each project. I pray for each of my clients. I have actually prayed for each person reading this book. I pray for God to sustain my health, the virality of my mind, and for the resources that my clients need to be successful. The power of prayer is evident in everything that I do because I do not believe that I can achieve anything without God's spiritual guidance and assistance. It was risky to include this chapter in the book because some people may see it listed first and become turned off. It may even stop some people from purchasing the book but that's ok because it would be disingenuous of me to say that God is the head of my life, the source of my strength, and the reason for all that I do but neglect to give him honor in this realm. Neglecting the role of prayer in my personal and professional life would be like neglecting a major part of who I am.

I am not going to preach to you in this chapter, but I will share how the power of prayer has helped me to reach success in my life. When I look over my resume, I honestly never set a goal to achieve half of the things that I have accomplished. My focus has always been to be a blessing in the lives of others and to pursue the purpose that God has for me.

I love the idea that America was founded on religious freedom. What that actually means, how that actually occurred, and is that actually happening is open for debate; however, one of the narratives that we were fed about the founding of this country is that religious freedom was important at the country's inception. For me, that means that each person has the right to believe in whatever they want to believe in. I must confess that I am a Christian minister and I feel compelled to introduce people to Jesus Christ, my Lord and Savior. However, I also recognize that there are other beliefs and there are those who simply don't believe.

When thinking about the power of prayer, don't limit this to the Christian context. Think about what helps to settle your mind when you feel anxious. For me, it's prayer. I have a little talk with Jesus about whatever is going on and I trust that after that talk everything will work out. Some people may scoff at this approach, but it has saved me plenty of moments that could have been filled with worry. When I am uncertain about a situation or how to deal with a problem, I think WWJD (What would Jesus do?). In the Christian faith, Jesus is the embodiment of love, not just love for yourself but love for your neighbors, love for your community, love for the less fortunate, love in all contexts. When I can't decide how I should proceed, I ask myself, how would Jesus show his love in this situation.

My prayer life is also strengthened in my refusal to believe that life is about me and my happiness. Yes, I derive happiness from the things that I feel blessed to do but most importantly, I recognize that I am a servant leader. I am called to serve the people who I lead. I don't expect them to give me any deferential treatment but to respect me as I respect them. My intent is to give as much or more than I receive from others. I want to be the blessing that someone woke up praying for. Without a strong prayer life, I would be more concerned with my personal circumstances, which are not always ideal, than with my desire to serve others. I use my power of prayer to remain centered during my personal storms so that I can keep my ship focused on reaching goals.

Whoever or whatever you worship or believe in should serve as a source of comfort, strength, and empowerment in your life. Developing this understanding will help you to understand your core value system. It will serve as your compass for future decision making. Are the plans that I have for my life, my family, and my work aligned with the type of person that I want to be? Am I making the types of decisions and living the kind of life that brings me peace? If you can not answer affirmatively, you may want to think about the power of your prayer life or your personal devotional time. This can be time spent reading the Bible, reading motivational quotes, or writing affirmations.

If it isn't already obvious, this is one of the first and most important keys to unlocking any power in your life. If you are not grounded and centered in who you are, it will be difficult to access power in the other areas of your life. Not impossible, but difficult because in some instances you may find yourself striving for goals that are not in alignment with what you really believe. In other instances, it may be because you are not totally convinced that the path you are following is leading to your purpose.

I can honestly share that I have not always been so secure with myself. I spent most of my adolescent years trying to fit in with others and doing things that I knew did not represent my personal value system. Even in the midst of doing them, I was having fun, but I knew I wasn't being true to myself. It was more important for me to fit in with a crowd than to walk the path that I knew had been created for me. Once I embraced the power of prayer and received assurance from God that I was created for a purpose, that every step of my life had already been preordained and all I needed to do was listen to his Word and walk in his will; I found my peace.

I'm southern, from a small town in southern Alabama that only people who have traveled south on Interstate 65 have heard of because they probably stopped at one of our fast food restaurants headed to the beach. Growing up in the south, I went to church a lot. I would hear the older people sing and hum and petition God for peace the surpassed all understanding. I had no understanding of what they were talking about because I didn't have a relationship with the God who could provide that. I thought I could create my own peace. I can laugh about that now because my attempt at creating peace was trying to control the things happening around me. I had expectations of how people should act and how events should unfold. I now know that I have no control over those things. I can only control me. I can control how I react to situations. I can control how I treat people. I can control where I invest my time and with whom. Those are things that I can do to create peace while trusting God to deal with the rest. Trust me. This wasn't an easy process, however, there is no way that I would be where I am if I had not gone through it.

You may be thinking that you don't know how to pray. It's much easier than you think because there honestly isn't a right or wrong way to do it. God wants to hear from us. He wants to have a relationship with us.

You may pray to God in adoration and worship. This is simply acknowledging his role and his greatness in your life. Have you ever driven through the mountains of Tennessee or sunk your feet into the warm sand of the tropical ocean? Have you ever noticed how the trees change with the seasons while remaining a source of strength and life on earth? Have you ever noticed the flowers that were once wilting now blooming when the sunlight penetrates them? The same God who created the majesty of the earth also created you. You are not an accident. That deserves a few moments of your time to just say, "thank you, God."

You may petition God. This is probably the type of prayer that many of us are most familiar with. We find ourselves in a jam and we don't know who else to turn to, so we call on The Lord. I can't speak for God, but I don't think he minds. We do have to realize that God's time is not our time so you can't make a petition and expect an immediate response. When you petition God, you have to trust that he has heard you and he will answer, in his time. Even when it feels like he hasn't heard you or he isn't listening, he is. As much as you may ask from him, do not be surprised if his answer does not come in the form that you expect. Sometimes those answers require us to change ourselves or our circumstances. Sometimes they require us to remain the situation longer than we would like so that we can learn the lesson.

We can also intercede on behalf of others. The ability to pray prayers of intercession are a sign of spiritual maturity. Many of us become so consumed with our own needs and desires that we forget to call the names and situations of others. I joke with my friends that I don't think I was a very good friend before my relationship with God developed. I thought I had all of the answers to fix their problems but once I unlocked my power of prayer, I realized that I could not only unlock it for myself, but I could talk to God about my friends, clients, and family members. Not to always ask for anything in particular but to let him know that they were on my mind and I was trusting him to show me how to be the blessing they may be praying for.

Prayers of thanksgiving are often overlooked in our daily hustle and bustle. I once read a quote that asked, "What if you only had the things today that you thanked God for yesterday?" If you take a moment and think about all of your blessings, great and small, you would develop an attitude of sincere gratitude. Our society is constantly evolving and developing something newer and better which keeps us striving for more and more but if we stop and think about what we have and what we have accomplished, we would be grateful for our current circumstance. We may not be where we want to be, but we are doing so much better than we could be. Have you thanked God that things are as well as they are?

Finally, we can give God praise! Your praise is not only about gratitude for God's love for you but a demonstration of your love for God. Don't be surprised if you start to praise God and find tears flowing from your eyes, a side to side sway of your body, a tapping of your foot, or even a low moaning because you don't have the words to describe what you are feeling. When you really think back to all God has done for you, you begin to thank him! I'm going to stop before I break out in my own praise break but giving God praise helps you to see how great his love is for you and should compel you to share that love with others.

Prayer is important because it helps us to live a grounded and centered life while also helping to guide our decision making. Take some time to recognize that just as the trees, flowers, and birds have a role to play in the majesty of the world, so do you. No matter what you choose to believe in, you should have confidence that your existence is not by accident and that you have a purpose in this world and in the lives of those around you.

Let's think about your prayer life...

Are the plans that I have for my life, my family, and my work aligned with the type of person that I want to be?

_____

_____

_____

Am I making the types of decisions and living the kind of life that brings me peace?

_____

_____

_____

What do I believe in?

_____

_____

_____

How do I measure what is right and wrong?

_____

_____

_____

What is important to me?

_____

_____

_____

What are my deal breakers?

_____

_____

_____

#PowerofP

What do I want people to think about me?

_____

_____

_____

How do I treat people?

_____

_____

_____

How do I want to be treated?

_____

_____

_____

Who do I go to for answers?

_____

_____

_____

How do I know when I am making the right decision?

_____

_____

_____

What am I thankful for?

_____

_____

_____

#PowerofP

Who can I pray for?

_____

_____

_____

Other Thoughts:

I will unlock the power of PRAYER by…

My vision for my prayer life:

My goal for my prayer life is:
(Is it SMART?)

Beginning today, I will:

"Too often we underestimate the power of a touch, a smile, a kind word, a listening ear, an honest compliment, or the smallest act of caring, all of which have the potential to turn a life around."

— Leo F. Buscaglia

UNLOCKING THE POWER OF PURPOSE

They say that the day you discover your purpose is one of the greatest days of your life. I could not agree more. Even though I don't actually remember the exact day, I remember the feeling. I remember feeling like, yes, I am finally doing what I am supposed to be doing. I remember realizing that my life and my work had finally become about more than earning an income or doing a job. I remember the excitement of knowing that my contributions to the world were actually having an impact. Maybe not the impact of curing cancer but the impact of a business owner realizing their profitability, a young adult developing a more fervent prayer life, a campaign team developing a winning strategy, an author opening their first box of books and seeing their work in print. Those moments are more valuable than any check that I have ever deposited. Don't get it confused. Money is necessary to sustain my lifestyle and to take care of my son but living in purpose is what drives me on those days when I want to give up or when the task becomes extremely frustrating.

Finding your purpose is like realizing why you were created. What a shame it would be to spend your entire life working for someone else's purpose and never realizing your own.

When I was growing up, I thought I wanted to be a lawyer. In fact, many people still think that I would make a great lawyer because I love to debate and try to advocate for the underdog, but it took me some time to realize that there are other ways to do that. It was hard not living up to the expectations of others but once I realized that I was living the life that I believe was created for me, it didn't matter whether others approved of my choices or not.

One of the most frequently asked questions that I receive is, "how do I know what my purpose is?" Unfortunately, that is a question that no one can answer for you. It is something that has to come from within. However, there are ways that you can arrive at the answer.

One method is to think about what you really love to do for others. One misconception that I feel people have about purpose is that it is all about us. I don't believe we were created to only benefit ourselves. I believe we were created to be a part of a community, to contribute to the community, and to make the community better. However, in the midst of serving, we should not be miserable. Our service should be rendered with joy. What makes you so happy that when you are doing it, you lose track of time? It may be visiting seniors at the assisted living facility, it may be working as a mentor to kids or young adults. If you look over your calendar and don't see anything that you are doing, absolutely love it, and lose track of time; replace some of those activities with new activities. Don't be afraid to volunteer with new organizations or switch to a different committee within your organization. Many times, our work feels like drudgery because we are not doing what we are purposed to do.

A common myth that I hear people spread is that your purpose should lead to profit or that you need to work in your purpose. That is not always true. Sometimes your purpose is a thing that you get to spend your evenings or weekends doing and there is no financial compensation attached, just the joy in your spirit knowing that you are making a difference and contributing to the community.

Back to the methods… second, ask yourself what you are really good at. It may be something that you can do with your eyes closed and you enjoy doing it. It could be as simple as creating spreadsheets. I bet you are like, *"LaKesha, you are crazy."* Whose purpose is creating spreadsheets? But think about it, if you really enjoy analyzing data, you can use those skills to volunteer with a local non-profit that needs help compiling data for a grant. So often, we neglect considering how we can be a part of something greater. Our purpose is not always this great or grand revelation, sometimes our purpose is to help someone else become great. Whew! That's tough because in many cases, we want to be great and acknowledged for the work that we do. However, we should also want to be a part of something great. I have worked with so many people who wanted to start a business or a not for profit, but they only possessed a few of the skills needed to be successful. We have to be willing to set ourselves to the side to find others who have the gifts that helps the team to be great and operate in its purpose or to become one of the persons who contributes to someone else's team becoming great.

Finally, think about what you are known for. What do people consistently seek you out for? Do you make cakes that everyone loves? In your mind, you're like that's not purpose, that's just something that I do but have you ever considered what happens to those cakes once they leave your oven. Of course, people eat them and love them, but have you imagined the smiles on their faces while they are sharing slices with family and friends. We often make the mistake of thinking that we have to see and experience the end results of our purpose. But whatever you were created to be or do, should first give you joy because you recognize how blessed you are to do it, but it should also give others joy, whether you get to witness the end result or not.

In my business, I know that my purpose is to give people advice based on the years of experience that I have attained and the variety of situations that I have found myself counseling about. Each occurrence was like a building block preparing me for the next. While operating in my purpose, I don't always get to see or even receive any credit for the role that I may have played in someone's long term success but that's ok because my purpose is not attached to their success. My purpose is to share the knowledge and wisdom that I have so that I can provide a building block in their process.

Your purpose should not solely be centered around building for others, but it should allow you to contribute meaningfully to others in a way that makes you happy and allows you to feel fulfilled. Once you share your purpose, you can't control where it goes or how it is received, and you have to be ok with that. Just as going to the assisted living facility may not elicit smiles from every resident, there will be some who will appreciate your presence. You may never meet every person who tastes your cakes but enjoy the smiles you are able to witness.

Many people miss finding their purpose because they are focused on profit. Take the finances out of the initial evaluation. Once you determine your purpose, then you can start to evaluate whether it can be monetized. For some people that may be an automatic yes. You are a whiz at helping people to organize their closets and people are willing to pay for it. For others, it may be coaching a little league sports team and you will spend more money than you will ever make. Either way, it is up to you to decide what you were meant to be doing while living this crazy thing called life.

When we are able to unlock the power of our purpose, we are able to freely share our gift with the community. Of course, this doesn't mean allowing people to take advantage of you. Knowing who and when to share with comes from your sense of discernment which is unlocked with your prayer life because God shows you who should be in your life and who he wants you to bless. However, when you are in the blessing business, you don't worry about rewards and recognition because knowing that you are doing what you are supposed to be doing is the greatest reward.

I have helped countless clients that I knew I wasn't being paid what my time was worth in the situation. I could have demanded more but my discernment told me to do the work and trust God. It has never failed that by following that advice, I was blessed in another area. Being centered and grounded when you are operating in your purpose will unleash a level of power and peace that cannot be described or compensated for. It will have you floating on cloud nine because there will be something on the inside of you that just knows, I am where I am supposed to be, and I am doing what I am supposed to be doing.

We will all die one day, and at the end of our lives people will not speak of the material possessions that we attained but they will speak of the quality of life we lived. They will speak of what your life meant to them. What a shame for us to walk through life never finding or living a life of purpose, but always seeking affirmation from others and working for financial gain. Make it your mission to live a life of purpose and service. It will not look the same for everyone so don't be afraid to blaze a trail on your journey to your purpose.

Let's think about your purpose...

What makes me so happy that when I am doing it, I lose track of time?

_____

_____

_____

What do people know me for?

_____

_____

_____

When do I feel most fulfilled?

_____

_____

_____

What makes me smile just thinking about it?

_____

_____

_____

How do I feel when I am helping others to become successful?

_____

_____

_____

What do I want my legacy to be?

_____

_____

_____

Other Thoughts:

#PowerofP

I will unlock the power of my PURPOSE by…

My vision of my purpose is:

My goal for finding my purpose is:
(Is it SMART?)

Beginning today, I will:

"This life is yours. Take the power to choose what you want to do and do it well. Take the power to love what you want in life and love it honestly. Take the power to walk in the forest and be a part of nature. Take the power to control your own life. No one else can do it for you. Take the power to make your life happy."

— Susan Polis Schutz

UNLOCKING THE POWER OF PASSION

Some people only think of passion in a romantic sense, however, passion is like fuel. It is an energy that excites and drives us. When we recognize what we are passionate about, we often see that they are things that we care the most about because you don't care about the things that don't matter.

When I was growing up, there were certain stories that my Grandmother would tell me over and over again. As I got older, I began to realize that those were issues that she was passionate about. She would tell those stories because they were replaying in her mind, they were issues that really bothered her, issues that she really cared about. When thinking about my passion, I often reflect on what is replaying in my subconscious.

What are the issues that bother me even when I am not consciously thinking about them?

What issues make me angry enough to want to do something about them?

At first, they were difficult questions to answer without some introspection because I wasn't taking the time to sit and listen to myself, to listen to the voice inside my own head. But once I identified the areas that I was passionate about, I was able to connect with volunteer organizations where I felt my skills were needed and where I could make a difference. I can commit to those organizations because they are engaged in work that I am passionate about.

My undergraduate degree is in Political Science. I thought it was by chance that I chose this degree. I was entering my junior year of college and was told that I needed to declare a major. I entered college as an Economics major but quickly realized that was not the lane for me. I spent the next few semesters touring the College of Arts and Sciences and taking classes in almost every discipline. When confronted with narrowing my scope to just one for the next year and a half, I looked at my transcript and chose the subject that I had the best grades – Political Science.

At the time, I didn't think too deeply about the decision but as I have gotten older, I have realized that that decision was my way of choosing what I was most passionate about. My political science classes were the ones that had readings that actually interested me and kept my attention. They were the papers that I enjoyed writing. My logical self would have asked what type of job did I expect to get with a Political Science degree but I was too excited that I had identified something I really enjoyed.

Almost twenty years later, I am still passionate about issues related to politics. I am fascinated with how voters internalize information to cast votes. I am deeply curious about the intersection of religion and politics. My pleasure reading typically involves books or articles related to politics. And of course, the issues that make my blood boil involve racial and economic inequalities.

Passion and purpose are often confused. In my personal definition, passion is how you feel, and purpose is what you do. Knowing what you are passionate about can sometimes lead to you discovering your purpose and vice versa.

When you are surfing online, what types of information do you gravitate toward? When you are talking to friends and family, what is the subject that causes your ears to perk up and your eyes to light up? When you are watching the news, what gets your attention and makes you feel like you want to do something?

Making the connection between your passion and your purpose will lead to fulfillment. You may be great at making floral arrangements. You could arrange flowers all day but arranging flowers for bridal shows versus creating them for individual clients can create different emotional responses. When someone discovers their passion such as making floral arrangements but don't take the time to understand their purpose, whose building blocks are these flowers for, they can find themselves operating in their purpose but not finding any joy.

It is obvious when you see people operating in their purpose with passion. They make the work look effortless and they find great joy with or without reward. It is equally obvious when people are operating in their purpose with no passion. They enjoy what they are doing but it feels pointless, they often question whether they are making a difference. Finally, it shows when a person is operating in their passion with no purpose. They are happy doing what they are doing but there is no measurable impact.

Do you find yourself in any of these three situations? If so, it is important to take some time to determine what you are passionate about and to connect that with your purpose. Can you imagine how powerful you will feel when you know that you are not only doing what you are meant to be doing but you can also feel how it is making a difference in your community?

We often desire that our children will find a good job, but I have changed my desire for my son. I pray that he will discover what he is passionate about and that he will find his purpose. It isn't hard to make a living when you know what you enjoy doing. You may not make millions of dollars, but you will find a way to earn enough for a place to live and food to eat. That may sound so strange because we have been conditioned to insert ourselves in the rat race of having a nice house, driving a fancy car, wearing designer clothes, and eating food that we can't pronounce. Have you noticed how many celebrities are battling depression and committing suicide? Many times, they have all of the things that we have been conditioned to chase. I don't know if it is because they are not getting therapy to deal with emotional issues or mental illness or if it is because they have not found their purpose and passion, but it should be evident that material success is not the answer to all of our problems.

Don't get me wrong, I am not ever going to encourage people to give it all up and slum for the good of the whole because there is nothing wrong with having nice things, but I am advocating for you to choose your purpose and passion over material things and watch how your perspective changes. So, don't go and quit your day job to pursue your passion but find ways to work to sustain your lifestyle while also spending time on the things that actually bring you joy and fulfillment. At some point, I would like to believe that your vocation will find an intersection with your passion and purpose.

Let's get practical and discuss some strategies that you can use to discover your passion.

What did you love doing as a child or when you didn't have to think about the responsibilities of adulthood? Just as I found my passion when I wasn't thinking logically, you may also find yours by throwing what you should be doing or what others expect you to be doing out of the window. Allow yourself to rewind to a time when you were free to daydream. Do you still enjoy doing it? Is this something that, even if you can't do it full-time, you can incorporate into your schedule?

Visualize your future. Again, dare to dream. If you could write your future from this moment forward without taking your past into consideration, what would it look like? What would you spend your time doing? Who would it benefit? How would it make you feel? Once you open your eyes, think seriously about the potential of making that vision a reality. What steps would you need to take today to begin creating that future? It may not happen overnight, but can you find the joy in taking the steps along the journey to get you to the space of living in your passion?

Try new things. You may be saying that you have never really felt passionate about anything and when you close your eyes, you don't see anything. That's not a problem. You need to be willing to expand your horizon at this point. Get out of your routine and try some new things. You will not only discover what you like, but you will also come across some things that confirm what you don't like.

Journal your thoughts. Just like my grandmother would rehash stories that stayed on her mind, after a few months of journaling, you should begin to see a trend in your writing. What are the subjects that you keep coming back to? Allow your thoughts to flow freely so that you can tap into your innermost thoughts and not the filtered, processed thoughts that lead to logical decisions.

Think about where you spend your time and money. I often tell clients that I can tell their organization's priorities by how they spend their time and their money. We invest in what is important to us. What do you read? Where do you like to go? What do you like to do? What do you enjoy talking about? Again, set aside the things on that list that aren't bringing you any joy or that you do to accommodate others. Let's focus on those things that you are doing for your own pleasure.

Hopefully, these exercises will serve as a starting point for you to unlock your passion. It is my goal for you to finish this book with a sense of power that you have never felt before. You can't find and feel that power without some passion fueling it.

Let's think about your passion...
What are the issues that bother me even when I am not consciously thinking about them?

_____

_____

_____

What issues make me angry enough to want to do something about them?

_____

_____

_____

What makes my blood boil?

_____

_____

_____

#PowerofP

What gets me so excited that my heart starts to beat fast?

_____

_____

_____

What do I surf for on the internet?

_____

_____

_____

What do I like to read or learn more about?

_____

_____

_____

Unlocking the Power of Passion

What do I like to talk about?

_____

_____

_____

What do I enjoy hearing other people talk about?

_____

_____

_____

What did I enjoy doing as a child?

_____

_____

_____

What do I see when I visualize my future?

_____

_____

_____

What new things am I willing to commit to trying?

_____

_____

_____

What do I journal about when I'm not filtering my thoughts?

_____

_____

_____

How do I spend my time and money?

_____

_____

_____

Other Thoughts:

#PowerofP

I will unlock the power of my PASSION by…

My vision of my passion is:

My goal for finding my passion is:
(Is it SMART?)

Beginning today, I will:

"Be not the slave of your own past – plunge into the sublime seas, dive deep, and swim far, so you shall come back with new self-respect, with new power, and with an advanced experience that shall explain and overlook the old."

– Ralph Waldo Emerson

UNLOCKING THE POWER OF YOUR PAST

I spent at least five years of my life in what felt like a haze. I was working and going through the motions of life, but I didn't feel like I was gaining any traction. Several years later, I looked back on that time period and realized that although I didn't understand why I was going through those motions, they were preparing me for the next chapter of my life.

It can be difficult to look at some of the situations that we go through and understand the impact they will have later in life but the experiences of yesterday will help to shape who we become tomorrow. Past experiences effect future decisions because we use that data to determine how we will react to situations that may be similar to something we have previously experienced.

Little did I know, those years that I felt like I was wandering through a haze were actually preparing me to become a Consultant. I was gaining the skills to be able to help business owners with a wide range of professional dilemmas.

Working as a waitress taught me the importance of having efficient processes. You can't go to a table and deliver their food without having already taken their food and drink order. Success is a process.

Yes, it takes time but if you skip a step, you will probably fail to reach your desired goal.

Working as a retail salesperson taught me the importance of understanding a client's needs. We have a temptation to give people what we want them to have but those usually result in returns. It is important to help people find what they love and that requires us to take more time to listen than speaking.

Working as a retail store manager taught me some very valuable lessons about human resources. I had to fire my first employee. I didn't want to, but my regional manager reminded me that this person was pulling my team down and if I didn't terminate him, his performance could eventually lead to my termination. As much as I wanted to protect the one worker, I had to consider the needs of the team as well as myself.

Finally, working as a licensed financial adviser taught me the importance of fiscal responsibility, not only in your personal life but also in your professional life. I worked with insurance and investment products which showed me how much the average American does not understand about finances while those who do understand are able to use leverage to create generational wealth. It was hard to have conversations with families about life after the death of one of the spouses or what would happen if they didn't save enough for their children to go to college or for their own retirement. However, my clients appreciated me presenting the worst-case scenarios to them so that they could see the potential pitfalls in their future. Too often, we seek the rose-colored advice rather than appreciating both sides of the story - how great life can become while also understanding what can potentially go wrong.

Ironically, to others, it seems like the knowledge comes naturally but that is only because of the information that I gathered from those past experiences. I see situations and they are familiar so I can use the lessons learned in the past to help someone else not make the same future mistakes. The years that I worked those jobs, even though they did not seem to be fulfilling my passion or purpose, they were preparing me for what was to come next.

I can also recall some personal experiences that were not so pleasant, but they helped to shape the person that I am today. I learned that without confronting those situations and honestly dealing with how they were impacting my present self, I was destined to stay in a cycle of making the same mistakes because as I was recalling data, I was processing the hurt instead of the lessons. The saying is true, hurt people hurt people and we sometimes bleed all over the people who had nothing to do without pain. I still carry some of the pain of my past, but I am aware of my triggers, so I don't allow my past hurts to impact decisions about my future.

There are some experiences in our past that we would prefer to forget.

(that sentence deserves to stand on its own)

However, we have to recognize that we are a sum of the experiences in our lives, good and bad. Not understanding how you got to where you are today, can make it hard to move forward in your life.

Have you ever met someone who was so stuck in their past that they expected every future situation to be like the one they experienced before? Not dealing with and understanding the many influences that have created our current situations cause us to be destined to make many of the same decisions again and again. From intimate relationships to personal relationships and choosing jobs, if we don't get to the root of the issue, it continues to manifest in different situations and different people.

In my opinion, this starts with childhood. Yes, you have to go all the way back. Look around at your family during that time, look at your friends, look at your school, your house. All of that data was inputted in your brain's data system to create the biases and understandings that you have today.

Let's take a look at what some may consider to be a controversial example. a racist.

When we look at their households, the persons that they spent time with growing up, their school environments, the values instilled as children, the messages communicated to them about "others;" we will understand, even if we don't agree, how they became who they are. When racial slurs are spoken in the home, it is natural to use them because that was the normal others were spoken about. When living in a monolithic community, it is natural to believe that those other people are foreign because they had no relation or experience to compare their data with. When only being taught history from a supremacist point of view, it is natural that they will feel a sense of superiority. Racial superiority at the expense of another's liberty and freedom is the lowest value system I believe a person can possess. The thought that others can be harmed or killed just because they are different from you is not something that can ever be tolerated. However, redemption is possible for these persons if they are willing to critically examine and confront the narratives that have fed into their belief system. Change is possible, but it must be intentional.

Each of our examples may not be as extreme but if we really look at our pasts, we can see some implicit biases that have been baked into our thinking about the world and about ourselves. What did you hear people telling you about yourself that you grew up to believe as truth? What did you hear people saying about your community that you believed to be true, whether factual or not? What did you hear people saying about the world that was either confirmed or debunked by personal experiences?

I know some people who won't eat food that they didn't eat growing up. If their momma or grandmama didn't serve it, at forty plus years old, they aren't eating it. This is not because they have ever had a bad experience with the new food type but simply because of the narrative that was embedded in their core memories. I have seen some of these same people try new foods from different cultures and love it. When they stepped outside of what had been programmed into them, they were able to create new data to process. Of course, I have also seen them try food that they hated. The difference is that they now hate the food because it does not taste good to them and not because that is the information that was programmed into them.

I know some people who were told that they would never amount to anything in life and they work every day to prove their haters wrong. This attitude can be equally motivating and destructive. It can motivate us to achieve more than we may have otherwise because we are determined to create a narrative that differed from what someone tried to impart onto us. However, it can also be destructive when we become so focused on proving others wrong rather than fulfilling our own passion. Our primary motivation in life should not be to make a point to others.

You can easily wake up one day at forty and realize you have charted a course that made a point but didn't make you happy.

It is important for us to critically analyze the things that have happened to us and the messages that we have been taught to determine if they are true and how they are impacting us. Some of them have made us better people while others have made us fearful of the world or fearful of other people without any justification.

Childhood molestation is one of the most disturbing occurrences in our communities that rarely receives any attention during childhood or adulthood. There are men and women carrying stores of past hurts and abuses that have impacted their ability to function in healthy adult relationships while others have become better parents because they were more vigilant about protecting their children than they would have been otherwise.

Whatever things you are carrying from your past, if you can't reconcile them on your own, see a therapist. I will say it again – See a therapist. There are trained professionals who are able to help you process data that your heart, mind, and soul don't know what to do with. Don't allow the traumas and pains of your past to hinder you from freely living into your future.

Unlocking the Power of Your Past

Growing up I told everyone that I wanted to be a lawyer. I don't even think I knew what a lawyer was or what they did aside from what I saw on television, but I would always get approving nods and words of affirmation when I boldly stated, I am going to be a lawyer! As I got older and realized that I hated reading legal briefs and memorizing case law, I had to accept that being a lawyer was probably not in my future. But, so much of my past identity was tied to, I am going to be a lawyer! I didn't know how to change my own narrative. I honestly don't think anyone cared that I didn't become a lawyer but my fear of disappointing all of those people who had given me the approving nods and words of affirmation kept me stuck and feeling like I was unsuccessful. If I had become a lawyer, I probably would have been an ok lawyer, but I definitely would not have been great because it would not have fueled my passion and it wasn't my purpose. Ironically, with a political science degree, I do have some connection to law so my childhood ideals were not too far off, but this example shows how you may have had some ideas about your future as a child, but you are not wedded to those narratives. You are free to create new paths each day based on old and new data.

Let's discuss a couple of strategies to deal with your past. First, think about the times in your past when you were the happiest. As we have previously discussed, these are breadcrumbs that lead to ideas of passion and purpose. Don't be afraid to ask family members and childhood friends about memories that they have of you when you were younger. Consider creating a chart beginning with the year you were born and narrating your life by chronicling major incidents that happened within the timeframes. This exercise should be an interesting way to understand how you have been influenced by incidents around the world as well as incidents within your family.

Second, what are some of the areas of your past that you wish you could forget? Rather than try to forget, I think it is time for you to focus on dealing with the issues. If you are not comfortable talking to someone, consider having a separate journal to deal with these issues. Some of the memories may be hazy from years of suppression. Writing them down will help to bring some clarity. I can not stress the importance of seeking professional help if the incidents are too difficult for you to resolve on your own.

Unlocking the power of your past can free you from some of the expectations that you may be carrying. It can also help you to identify the happiest moments of your life. We can not change our past but if we are not careful and intentional about how we process incidents that have occurred in our lives and around our lives, we may find ourselves repeating destructive habits.

Let's think about your past...
Description of my childhood.

_____

_____

_____

What was my family life like?

_____

_____

_____

What did I do after school?

_____

_____

_____

What was school like?

_____

_____

_____

What types of people did I hang around?

_____

_____

_____

What types of food did I like to eat?

_____

_____

_____

Unlocking the Power of Your Past

Where were my favorite places to go?

_____

_____

_____

What did I want to become?

_____

_____

_____

What was my first sexual encounter like?

_____

_____

_____

#PowerofP

What were my thoughts about people unlike myself?

_____

_____

_____

How did I determine what I would do after high school?

_____

_____

_____

What is the most painful memory from my past?

_____

_____

_____

Unlocking the Power of Your Past

What is the most pleasant memory from my past?

_____

_____

_____

What from my past motivates me?

_____

_____

_____

In what areas do I feel stuck?

_____

_____

_____

#PowerofP

What is one thing I would like to talk to a therapist about?

_____

_____

_____

What am I holding on to from my past that I want to let go of?

_____

_____

_____

Other Thoughts:

Unlocking the Power of Your Past

#PowerofP

I will unlock the power of my PAST by…

My vision for dealing with my past:

My goal for dealing with my past:
(Is it SMART?)

Beginning today, I will:

#PowerofP

"Persistence. Perfection. Patience. Power. Prioritize your passion. It keeps you sane."
— Criss Jami

UNLOCKING THE POWER OF THE PAUSE

You are exactly where you are supposed to be.

After the birth of my son, I decided to not work for the first year of his life so that I could be present for him. As wonderful as this sounds, it was one of the hardest years of my life. I was so accustomed to being in a state of doing that I had a hard time pausing to be present. This continues to be a struggle that I wrestle with, even in my daily life.

Taking the time to stop and be still can be difficult. Using this time allows us to hear from God because the power of our prayer is not only in speaking to God but also hearing from God. It also allows us to find our passion, to take the time to hear what excites and upsets us. In a society that provides 24-hour access to almost anything that you want, it can be difficult to turn it all off and just be. If I am not careful, I will wake up checking my social media, jump right into my day checking the news, start client calls and checking emails, wind down listening to a book, and go to bed listening to a movie that I have seen a million times (my way of not staying up to see what is going to happen in the end, lol). I have to be conscious about taking some time to turn everything off, set my phone to the side, and just be still.

One of my struggles with the pause was feeling like I was going to miss something. Sounds crazy but sometimes we act like if we miss a meeting, miss a day on social media, or don't decide fast enough then we are somehow missing out on a big moment or opportunity but taking some time to rationally think and reflect will help you to develop clarity of thought. I have taken breaks from social media and guess what, I don't think any of my friends or followers left. They were still there when I came back. I have turned off the news and the pundits were still there when I turned it back on. I have taken a day to respond to an email and the recipient did not seem to be bothered. Taking the time for myself allowed me to be in a better place because I took that time to center myself and ensure I was focusing on the things important to me rather than getting caught up on the hamster wheel of life's expectations.

Pausing is also something that I have to practice for my son. It amazes me how quickly he is growing up. I embarrass him with stories from his toddler years and all of the fun things that we did together. If you know anything about teenagers, you know that this is not their favorite topic of conversation. However, it is hard to imagine that this little person who used to depend on me for everything is now a man-child with a growing mustache. He doesn't want to spend as much time with me as he did when we would snuggle on the couch and watch his favorite cartoons and movies, so I have to be conscious of pausing when he does enter the room and wants to tell me a story or share a joke with me. The temptation can be to tell him to hold on while I finish what I am doing but I remind myself that the work will be there, the moments with him are fleeting. Pausing to be present for his stories and jokes is one of the keys to us staying connected.

Stop!

Close your eyes and count to 20.

What did you see? How did you feel? What were you thinking about? Did those 20 seconds seem to last a lifetime?

If so, you need to spend more time practicing the pause. Take some time to be silent and to focus on... nothing. Clear your mind and take time to allow new ideas, new thoughts, and new energy to enter. We spend so much time focused on getting from here to there, going from this to that, and we rarely give ourselves the space to reflect and reset.

My year away from business gave me a chance to see the work that I was doing with a fresh perspective. It helped me to see what I really missed doing, which led me to understand my purpose. Seeing what I enjoyed doing even when I wasn't being paid showed me what I was passionate about. Most importantly, becoming a mother caused me to confront a lot of my past ideas about life to determine what kind of future I wanted to create for my son. If I had gone from working to motherhood and straight back to working, I probably would have kept the same type of job and continued the work that I was doing before. I understand that not everyone has the luxury of taking a whole year off and I was only able to do so because I moved back home with my mom (thank you, mommy). But the point is that we all need to take some time whether 20 seconds, one weekend, or a full day to exhale all of the thoughts, plans, and to-dos that are swimming around in our heads and allow ourselves to inhale some new ideas, new dreams, and new goals.

Have you ever looked at the clock or calendar and wondered where time has gone? This often happens when we don't take the time to stop and smell the roses or live in the moment. Life is too short to allow it to fly by while you are running on the hamster wheel. Look at your calendar and see if you are scheduling time to pause. Are you planning time to eat every day? Are you planning time to get up and walk around your office or even outside for a few minutes? Have you scheduled almost every minute of your day until you go to bed tired and wake up tired? If so, you need to take better care of yourself and look for times to pause.

Be intentional about how you spend your time. Be intentional about who you spend your time with. Don't feel like you have to respond to everything, immediately. The power of the pause can also be a conflict resolution tool. How often have you been so quick to respond in a situation that you regretted your response because you didn't take the time to think through what you should have said? I have coached many clients through my communication training on how to deal with difficult people by practicing the pause. When someone reacts irrationally, you don't have to react in the same way. Take a moment to think through your response. Take a moment to allow them to sit with their behavior. The power of your pause means that you are able to control your emotions rather than being reactive. It may infuriate the person attempting to engage with you, but it will center you. Your pause will allow you to craft a calm and rational response rather than adding gas to an already lit fire.

Let's try again.

Close your eyes and count to 20.

Were you able to release a little more? The more you try this, the more you will release. You may even find yourself setting aside dedicated time to pause and clear your mind. You may find yourself sitting outside on a warm day with your head held back, eyes closed, allowing the sun to infuse your mind with ideas and goals that you had long forgotten about. You may find yourself in a crowded waiting room clasping your hands in your lap as you close your eyes and allow yourself to drift into the realm of new realities. You may decide to take time at some points in your day to take a short walk to clear your head.

Every new invention, every innovation, every improved process had to be imagined before it could be created. It is really hard to daydream in the midst of busy. Some people think that daydreaming in a waste of time but when focused it can produce novels, stage plays, trips to the moon, or peace of mind. What ideas have you had but didn't do anything with because you were too busy with life to sit down and develop a strategy for implementation? Countless clients have come to me with projects that have been in their head for years, but they were too busy to work on them. I can't promise that these ventures will be profitable, but do you think they are worth exploring? Could they possibly lead to you discovering your passion or purpose?

When you unlock the power of your pause, you are unlocking a level of your mind that often gets pushed to the side for more practical and immediate thinking. Your pause helps you to become comfortable with yourself, in the moment. Not wanting anything, not racing toward the next thing, just being in the moment. I have found people to be uncomfortable with silence because they are not accustomed to being alone with themselves. They have been conditioned to fill time with noise.

Unlocking the power of your pause is also a form of self-care. It is showing yourself that you value your own voice and opinion. It helps you to become comfortable in your own skin. There is power in being able to stand alone and feel okay. As simple as that seems, it can be a struggle. Once you are able to master it, you will achieve a peace that no one can penetrate, and you will hear things that you have missed before. Because our minds are conditioned to swirl with multiple thoughts at once, we often don't hear what someone else is saying because we are either thinking of a response or thinking about something else. However, when you have learned to settle your mind, you can focus in on what people are saying to hear their intent, to observe their body language, and to respond based on what you are hearing and not what you are thinking. Active listening sounds easy, but an alarming number of high-level communicators are not good listeners. As you are working to unlock all of the powers necessary to become successful, it is imperative that you learn to listen to others and to yourself.

Let's think about your pause...

Where am I happiest?

___

___

___

When was the last time I did something for myself, by myself?

___

___

___

How comfortable am I in my own skin?

___

___

What are some goals, dreams, or ideas that I have packed away because they weren't practical, or I didn't have time?

_____

_____

_____

How comfortable am I in silence?

_____

_____

_____

How do I care for myself to ensure my mind, body, and spirit are grounded and centered?

_____

_____

Unlocking the Power of the Pause

What can I change in my daily routine to provide a few minutes of centering for myself?

How well do I listen to others?

How do I react when I don't feel like I am being heard?

#PowerofP

_____

How well do I handle conflict?

_____

_____

_____

Other Thoughts:

Unlocking the Power of the Pause

I will unlock the power of my PAUSE by...

#PowerofP

My vision for using my pause:

My goal for using my pause:
(Is it SMART?)

#PowerofP

Beginning today, I will:

Unlocking the Power of Your Presence

> "When your desires are strong enough, you will appear to possess superhuman powers to achieve."
>
> — Napoleon Hill

UNLOCKING THE POWER OF YOUR PRESENCE

When I have a meeting scheduled or a speaking engagement booked, my first thought is always, "What am I going to wear?" This may seem strange because some people think about the agenda or the project before them, but I always think about how I am going to show up.

Showing up is about more than walking in a room. It's about walking in the room with a level of confidence that requires everyone in the room to pay attention to you whether you are speaking or not. I am the representation of my brand. When people see me, they make instant assumptions about my ability to contribute to the conversation, my level of knowledge about my subject matter, and whether they trust me. Therefore, my concern is not which designer I am going to wear or how much my clothes cost but what can I wear to make me comfortable in my own skin so that I can show up as my authentic self. I want to be as comfortable as possible so that I can focus on being the best salesperson for my brand. A few questions that I ask are:

Will I be sitting or standing?

Will I be doing a lot of walking?

Will I be seated among a group or in the front of the room?

What is the age demographic of the crowd?

What are the cultural norms of the group?

What is the subject matter that I am representing? Business? Ministry? Young professionals?

Although it's good to stand out, I never want to stand out in a way that will make me uncomfortable or that will make those around me uncomfortable. I don't want to blend into the crowd, but I also don't want to look as if I don't belong. Spending time thinking through those things and investing in smart wardrobe pieces to accommodate most environments helps me to present my business and my brand in the best light.

The most important piece of my ensemble is my personality. Some may say that I am feeling myself right now but hear me out… I try to be the person that I would want someone else to be to me. Once you get past the exterior, which is important because people judge you based on your appearance, (that's a fact of life), they want to know what kind of person you are.

How are you showing up?

Are you flawless on the outside but falling apart on the inside?

You should know by now that I don't believe in faking it until you make it. If you need help to get your inside to match the outside, get help. It took me some time to come to this level of awareness because it was easier to pretend to be the person that everyone expected me to be but that seemed to make everyone happy but me.

Honestly, there are some days when I am not feeling it. I am not feeling leaving home. I am not feeling interacting with people. I just don't want to do it. And honestly, unless I'm being paid to show up, I stay home. I would rather get myself together at home than to be out in public looking or acting crazy. If it is somewhere that I have to be, I take time to pause and determine why I am feeling the way that I am feeling. I engage in self-talk to build myself up for the occasion. I don't want to be fake. I don't want to have to pretend. I want to be genuinely excited to be wherever I am going. I want to be in the moment. I want to enjoy the conversation and make meaningful connections. If I can't do that, why bother?

I do giggle a little when people compliment me or say things like, you always dress so nicely because they don't know (or they didn't until now) how important my appearance is to my ability to be present. If my shoes are hurting my feet or skirt is too tight, that becomes my focus and not what is happening around me. I remember going to a book signing and the zipper on my skirt busted on my way to the event. I knew that the skirt was a bad choice, but it was so cute and had arrived the day before my flight which left no time for an exchange at the store. Against my better judgment, I wore it. Luckily, I was wearing a shirt that could cover where it had busted but throughout the book signing, I was focused on my busted zipper. Although I was selling books, having conversations with people, and taking pictures; in the back of my mind, I was focused on the busted zipper. I was paranoid that someone would notice. Fortunately, we were in a location where I could get another skirt before heading to my next event, but the incident reminded me of the importance of my presentation when I show up.

I am going to go out on a limb and assume that if you are reading this book, you are considered a leader in some area of your life. Not just because leaders are readers but also because most leaders have a desire to unlock their hidden powers and to become better at whatever they choose to do. As such, there are probably people watching your every move (not literally) because they have an interest in what you are doing. Showing up in spaces as your authentic self is a sign of liberation and it is addictive. People gravitate toward free thinkers who aren't afraid to challenge the status quo or who dare to wear yellow pants with a denim top instead of denim pants and a yellow top. People are attracted to people who walk into a room apologetically. They don't have to say a word or create a scene but when they enter, the air feels different. You cannot help but notice them. Some call it confidence while others misinterpret it as arrogance, but I call it peace.

Owning who you are gives you a sense of peace. No matter what your personal or professional title is, when you are at peace with who you are and how you show up, you exude a quiet confidence derived from inner peace. You would be amazed at how many people aspire to attain this level of peace, but they can't find it because they haven't discovered their purpose or passion. They aren't comfortable with their past, so they try to mask it as something other than what it is, and they feel like they have to fill awkward silences with even more awkward words. However, people who have peace can be present in the moment. When they show up, they show feeling comfortable and confident. When they speak, they speak with a level of depth and clarity that makes others lean in to pay attention to what they are saying. They are able to listen intently to the conversations happening around them and contribute their thoughts to stimulate conversation.

This comfort and confidence does not manifest when you enter the doors of a location. You have to cultivate it in your private time for it to be authentic in front of others. I have seen people in some of the most expensive clothes and shoes who are obviously not comfortable with themselves, so they try to cover it up with clothes. Most people probably don't notice because they are in the hustle and bustle of trying to mask their own stuff, but it is very unfortunate to witness. I have also been around people who think that being the center of attention by being loud or demanding attention is a sign of confidence. It is actually a sign of insecurity. If you have to make a scene or create a commotion to get people to notice you, you are doing it wrong. The type of attention that you seek will not be generated using these methods. In most cases, people will notice you but they not be interested in genuinely getting to know you or engaging with you.

Knowing yourself is a very powerful tool. It prevents you from being defined by others or from having your past used against you. You recognize that you are a sum of your past experiences, but you are ok living in the moment and confident about the future, no matter what it holds. It gives you interesting things to talk about because you have read books and articles about things that you are passionate about so when you start speaking and your eyes start to light up, you pull people into the conversation. You are secure in your value system and able to stand firmly on your decisions whether others approve or not. People take notice and treat you with the respect that this level of self-valuation deserves.

You're probably thinking that you do that now but are you? I can honestly say that I'm still working on this. I still wonder if people will accept me. Will they like me? Will they want to work with me? Will they think I'm good enough? Will I say anything meaningful? I pray that God places those who should be in life in my path. I trust that God has placed in my path those who need my building blocks and those I can contribute building blocks to. I bring my best self into the room. I am ok being with the group but if I need to stand alone, that's ok too.

Unlock the power of your presence by imaging how you want others to see you. Start from your head and go all the way down to your shoes. This is not about becoming vain but getting comfortable in your clothes so that you show up as your best self.

Begin by thinking about your wardrobe. Do your clothes fit properly? If not and you can't afford a new wardrobe, consider getting them altered for a more customized fit. It's far less expensive than buying new garments, especially if you love the pieces. However, hanging on to ill-fitting clothes means you are either not wearing them or you look a hot mess when you go out. Neither is acceptable.

Based on your industry and networking circle, you should have basics that will flow from day to night. Men should always have a few well-tailored suits made from quality fabrics. You can use shirts and ties to dress up or dress down the suits. Women can invest in suits as well but having tops and bottoms that can be mixed will often provide more variety.

Next, examine your shoes. Are the heels or toes scuffed? Do they fit comfortably? Which shoes are better for walking than standing? Are the styles current? If not, is that a part of your signature look? Do you have the staple colors – black and brown/nude?

Do you have good hygiene? Of course, you are thinking that you can't believe I am even asking this question, but it is serious. If you sweat profusely, consider keeping extra shirts in your car or antiperspirant in your bag. If you know that your breath isn't always fresh, keep mints in your pocket (we are too old to chew gum at public events). Are your nails manicured? You don't have to go a salon but making sure you clean under your nails and avoid jagged edges will keep people from wincing when you reach out to make their acquaintance.

In my opinion, hair and make-up are very subjective. Don't be afraid to try new looks but be sure you are comfortable with the looks and not attempting to be trendy. If you opt for a more creative look, do not be surprised when people take notice of those elements. You want to stand out but not be a distraction.

You may need some help with this one but what do you sound like? I know people who don't like speaking in public because they don't like the sound of their voice. That can be problematic if you are trying to show up authentically and represent your brand. You need to be able to verbally communicate with confidence. Unless you can afford a sales team or a spokesperson, it is on you to sell the brand. Consider recording yourself speaking to determine what you don't like. Is it your word choice? If so, practice your public speaking by reading out loud and making mental corrections, even in casual conversations, when you revert back to your previous speaking patterns. Is it your pitch? Believe it or not, there are exercises that you can practice to adjust your speaking voice. You can also join speaking groups like Toastmasters or work with a speaking coach if you are interested in perfecting your public speaking.

Most importantly, do the internal work. So much of what is projected externally is a result of what is happening internally. From our attitude to our weight gain to our biases about being around certain people and eating certain foods. Be honest about what is stopping you from showing up authentically and start doing the work to improve or correct it. Don't be one of those people who shows up bleeding all over people because you don't want to bandage your wound.

When you unlock the power of your presence, you not only allow yourself the opportunity to connect with others, but you also demonstrate your ability to be a leader. As previously stated, people make instant assumptions about you based on what they see. They look at you and determine whether they trust the words that will follow. They decide if they want to do business with you and if they are interested in hearing more about your product/service. As the representative for your brand, you want people to lean in when you begin to present.

Finally, your presence has the power to encourage others to live in their truth. When people see the liberation that you have gained from being your goofy, funny, nerdy, sexy, or however you choose to show up self; they are also able to let down their guard and live in their truth. This level of freedom will lead to some of the best conversations and interactions that you may ever have. Rather than having meaningless small talk, you will find yourself engaging in deep meaningful interactions that often lead to long last relationships forged over common interests.

Let's think about your presence...
What is my most comfortable outfit?

_____

_____

_____

What items do I need to add to my closet?

_____

_____

_____

What items do I need to get rid of?

_____

_____

_____

Which items would benefit from a trip to a tailor?

Which shoes are best for walking?

Which shoes will only last about thirty standing minutes?

When was the last time I owned a room – walked in without a care in the world yet filled with confidence?

_____

_____

_____

What is stopping me from showing up authentically?

_____

_____

_____

How will being comfortable with myself attract others to me?

_____

_____

_____

#PowerofP

Other Thoughts:

I will unlock the power of my PRESENCE by...

My vision of my presence:

My goal for my presence:
(Is it SMART?)

Beginning today, I will:

"Recognizing power in another does not diminish your own."
— Joss Whedon

UNLOCKING THE POWER OF PARTNERSHIP

When I first started online networking almost 15 years ago, I formed some great partnerships with like-minded persons. We didn't have any written agreements, but we supported each other, cheered each other along, and would help to promote each other's projects. It is amazing to look back on those relationships to see how far we have come. A lot of people are afraid of partnerships because they think someone is going to steal their idea or try to compete with them.

I have rarely seen a McDonalds that did not have a Wendy's or Burger King in close proximity. Competition makes you better. Partnerships make you stronger. I see new Consultants and Professional Speakers/Trainers enter the market every day. Some of them reach out to me for advice on getting started or growing their business. I never shy away from sharing information because I know that no one can service my clients or deliver a presentation the way I can. I know what I bring to the table and I have confidence in my purpose and passion. This allows me to refer business to other people, to bring in other professionals on projects, and to share knowledge to help them become better.

Working together works.

I will admit that I didn't always think like this. There was a period in my teenage years when I had a hard time building and maintaining friendships. It wasn't about the other people. They were very fine people (lol). The problem was within me. I was insecure. I didn't think that I was pretty. I hated being a nerd, so I tried to be cool, but it didn't feel natural. I was pretending to be someone I wasn't so that I could fit in. Little did I know, if I had just shown up as myself, I probably would have had more friends and developed better relationships.

My best friend and I met through social networking before social media was really a thing. We would text each other all day, and we still do. She taught me how to be a friend. I went ghost on her a few times. Things got really crazy in my life and I reverted to my old habits. Retreat. She had to gather me and let me know that as my friend, she was going to show up for me and go through whatever I was going through with me. Even if I don't tell her exactly what's going on, I learned how to take off the mask and let her know when I wasn't ok. That's what a real partnership or friendship looks like. It doesn't matter if it's your best friend, the person you are in a relationship with, or a business vendor; be real about who you are and what you are capable of. Most people are going through their own thing so they will understand.

The situation with my best friend also taught me what I needed to do to be a better partner. Just as she is willing to show up for me, I am willing to show up for her. This lesson has spilled over into so many of my other relationships. I no longer worry if I am enough because I trust that the people I am supposed to be in partnership will accept the authentic me.

Relationships are hard. Not just dating or marital relationships but business relationships, family relationships, and relationships with friends. They are hard because they require an investment of time and energy and they require us to give as much as we receive. Many relationships suffer because one person is not willing to contribute at the level that they expect to receive.

Whether you are establishing a business partnership or seeking someone to date, you should not only consider what is in it for you and how you will benefit but also consider what you bring to the table for the other person. How are they benefiting from having you in their life? Aside from your winning personality, are you available to listen as much as you talk? Do you enjoy doing the things they want to do, or do you only want them to do what you want to do?

Asking yourself these questions can help you to determine if you are building meaningful and long-term partnerships. One of the keys to any successful partnership is communication. However, communication is hard when you are not comfortable with who you are. You can't have deep, meaningful interactions if you are only willing to skim the surface because your guard is up. Unfortunately, many of us have become accustomed to presenting our representative to those we meet. We have become adept at figuring out what people want and expect from us and in many situations, we should up to fulfill their expectation so that we can be accepted. This only works for a short period of time because our true personalities will eventually begin to show.

Before we leave the communication bit, I do have to caution you about discernment. You have to know who you should tell what. Not everyone should be privy to everything in your life. Some people call it keeping it real but to me it screams, I need therapy. If you find yourself telling your story to everyone you meet without vetting their character and intentions in your life, your overcommunication is probably a result of a need that you have to release but that release needs to come in a constructive environment that leads to healing. Sitting in a doctor's office and telling the person next to you all of your business is not constructive nor healing. This doesn't mean you should be ashamed of your testimony but there should be some discretion. When is the right time to share your testimony? When you have healed and learned the lesson from whatever you have gone through. If you are still processing and figuring out what happened, that is probably not the best time to share.

Trust is another key to successful partnerships. It is hard to trust others if you don't trust yourself. Trusting yourself means you are able to listen to your own voice, follow your own conscious, and feel confident in your decisions. It requires you being grounded and centered, understanding your purpose, knowing what you are passionate about, and feeling confident in your own skin. Will you always make the right decisions? No! We all make mistakes but trusting in our selves means we are willing to move forward and own that mistake. Lacking trust in yourself often results in you imitating the actions of others, being envious of others, and even deferring your life decisions to others. This makes establishing a partnership difficult because you are not bringing yourself into the equation. You are bringing a representative who will only be able to sustain the role for a short period of time.

If you have trust issues, like many of us, you have to get to the root of your issue. What disappointment led you to believe that others would disappoint you? What hurt led you to believe that others would hurt you? Understanding the root of the issue is not only beneficial in relationships but it also helps us to become better people. It helps us to recognize our triggers. We can see what types of situations might cause us to flinch or feel uncomfortable. Too often we ignore that feeling or repress the unpleasant things that have happened to us and end up making the same mistakes with different people. As we previously discussed, there is power in unlocking and understanding your past.

Finally, being supportive is a key element to any successful partnership. Many partnerships, especially business partnerships, fall apart because of the unwillingness or inability of one partner to hold up their end of the deal. This can be true in romantic relationships as well. For the most part, we begin relationships with the best intentions and present our best selves. However, when that best self and those good intentions are not authentic but are a representation of who or what we want to be, we are unable to maintain the mask. The unmasking of our true selves erodes trust because the other person becomes confused about who you really are. It is better to show up authentically and take the chance that the relationship will not work out than investing time and resources in a sham.

Most people enter relationships thinking WIIFM – what's in it for me? But I challenge you to examine your relationships and ask what am I contributing to this person's life or to this business deal? You should not only understand what you will be receiving but what do you have to offer. So often, I have seen clients approach potential sponsors and business deals knowing exactly what they want from the partnership but having no idea what they are willing or able to provide in return. I have seen countless singles seeking a mate with a list of attributes that they desire without asking if they have attributes that are compatible with their desires. When you think of the most successful relationships in your life, you will probably be able to see what you are getting from that person in your life as well as what you are giving. If not, you should ask yourself if the relationship is really what you think it is.

Unlocking the power of partnership requires you to look at each relationship as a two-way street. You should always be asking what you are getting as well as what you are giving and seeking to have balance. Of course, life happens and sometimes you will find yourself giving more than you are receiving or even receiving more than you are giving. However, the relationship should not be permanently one-sided. We all have some people who we have invested more into than they have reinvested in us. I am not advocating cutting those people off because sometimes our giving fills a need within us but if you find yourself giving begrudgingly, that is a problem. Also, think about those relationships where you may be getting more than you are giving. Consider being the one to call first, text first or even offer to pay for the next meal when you go out.

It is never too late to repave the road and put a relationship under construction while you work to add a second lane. This may look like you telling the person in your life that you need more from them because you feel like you are giving more than you are receiving or it may look like you doing more to be a better partner.

Let's talk about the type of people you need in your life. In your personal life, you need to have at least three types of people in your circle – someone who inspires you to dream your wildest dreams, someone who holds you accountable to the goals you set for yourself, and someone who isn't afraid to tell you the truth. In many instances, one person may embody one or more of these characteristics, but it is important to have these elements present in the people closest to you.

Having someone who encourages you to dream your wildest dream will push you to never settle. They will be the person who no matter how crazy your goal is, they will tell you to shoot your shot. The person who holds you accountable is going to ensure you are doing what you said you were going to do and being who you said you wanted to be. This person will remember your resolution to work out and ask when the last time was you went to the gym. They are important because they truly want to see us succeed and will ensure we are setting realistic goals. Finally, the person who tells you the truth is the person that you can always count on to shoot it to you straight, no chaser. This is the best person to go to for advice because unlike the dream supporter who will encourage you to do whatever you imagine possible or the accountability partner who will focus on the results; the truth teller is going to give you their unfiltered opinion. It may sting sometimes, and you may even feel like the person is being a hater but if the person really cares about you, value their truth-telling and analyze it to see if there is validity in what they are saying.

Professionally, you need seven people on your team – an attorney, an accountant, a financial adviser, a banker, a mentor, a coach, and a photographer. It is hard to deny that individuals are becoming mini corporations. As you seek to make your side hustle a business venture or to climb the corporate ladder, you have to realize that you can't do it alone.

You need an attorney, first and foremost, to ensure that the moves you are making are legitimate. You may not pay a monthly retainer for legal services, but you should have someone in your network who you can consult with before signing contracts or agreements and ensure you are properly entering and existing professional deals. A contract is only as good as your ability to enforce it. When having people sign confidentiality agreements and non-disclosure agreements, you should have some idea of what it will cost to enforce those documents if they are breached. Attorneys are not generally one size fits all so your main attorney may have to refer you to someone to handle specialized issues such as estate planning or civil litigation.

Your accountant should not only be available to assist with preparing tax filings but should also be consulted before entering business deals to ensure you understand how your financial situation will change. Not only can certain deals require your tax bracket to increase but they may also provide opportunities for the tax sheltering of funds.

As a former financial adviser, I cannot stress how important working with a financial adviser is. Even if you think you don't have enough in assets to hire a firm, go to your local bank, and ask if they have advisers on staff. This person should be able to assist with college planning and retirement planning along with any other long-term financial goals that you have. Most people think they don't make enough money to save but the reality is that we can and should do a better job with our spending. Your adviser can also consult on your asset allocations through your corporate retirement plan. If you are self-employed, working with an adviser should be mandatory because you don't have a company offering a benefits package therefore, you have to create it for yourself.

You should have a relationship with your banker. In the age of online banking and financial transactions, many people have no need to enter their financial institution until they need a loan. Developing a relationship with your banker prior to your need can help with planning for your short-term financial goals. Allowing them to understand your financial situation and what you are trying to achieve in the near term – buying a house or a car – will allow them to give you advice to prepare for the loan application and sometimes they may be able to serve as advocate once the document has been submitted.

Your mentor is not your best friend. A mentor is someone who has achieved a level of success that you would like to achieve in your own life. They will probably not spend hours on the phone with you or hang out with you, but they will be willing to share resources and contacts to help you achieve your goals. Typically, the more successful the person, the more limited their time will be so value the opportunities that you have with them. Be prepared with questions and know what you need from them. They will not have any problems telling you what they can and cannot do for you. Take their advice constructively because they probably don't have the time to sugarcoat their answers and are giving you information that they think will help you. It's ok not to agree but don't be argumentative. Take what you need and store away the rest. It will probably come in handy later.

Your coach is someone who will help you game plan your life. Much like a mentor, a coach is someone who you connect with on a more regular basis and they are usually willing to invest more time in the details of your goals. Unfortunately, life coaches and business coaches are sprouting up like weeds on social media so you should be very careful about who you select. Spend some time stalking their social media and connecting with other people they have worked with to get a feel for their services and the type of relationships they establish. Some coaches have programs and only work through groups while others offer one on one services as well as group programs. Just as anyone can coach a sports team, life and business coaches are the same. Many can get you in the game but not all will be able to get you to the championship. The person that you chose should have some demonstrative ability to help you achieve your goal and you should be willing to invest your time and financial resources to work with them. Many will offer a complimentary consultation to determine if there is a basis to work together. If so, you should expect to pay a fee for ongoing services. Some will charge a small fee for the initial consultation to ensure you are serious about moving forward.

Having a photographer on your team may seem like a waste but as you are building your brand, you will need to have regular professional photographs taken. There is nothing worse than looking at someone's LinkedIn profile or company website and seeing a camera phone picture, no image, or their logo icon. Invest in your image. You want to present yourself as someone others want to get to know. Working with a professional photographer once or twice per year will ensure you have quality images to update across your networks.

Unlocking the power of your partnerships will provide you with a group of people who can offer the support needed to move you closer to your goals but be mindful that these relationships are two-way streets. In our personal relationships, we should be considerate of how much time and energy we are reinvesting while in our professional relationships, we have to realize that services cost money.

After all, this is the livelihood for these persons and as great as you are, they are trying to build a business.

Let's take a look at your partnerships...

Who am I currently working with to help me become successful?

_____

_____

_____

What are some professional relationships that no longer serve me or my brand?

_____

_____

_____

Who needs to be added to my team?

_____

_____

_____

Where do I network?

_____

_____

_____

How often do I attend networking events?

_____

_____

_____

What is my goal for attending networking events?

_____

_____

_____

What is my relationship with my family like?

_____

_____

_____

Who are my three closest friends?

_____

_____

_____

What is my relationship with each of them?

_____

_____

_____

What can I do to ensure healthy relationships with my family and friends?

Do I have trust issues?

If so, what incident or incidents created my trust issues?

_____

_____

_____

What do I need to do to heal?

_____

_____

_____

Other Thoughts:

Unlocking the Power of Partnership

#PowerofP

I will unlock the power of my PARTNERSHIPS by…

My vision of my partnerships:

My goal for my partnerships:
(Is it SMART?)

Beginning today, I will:

"Power isn't control at all — power is strength and giving that strength to others. A leader isn't someone who forces others to make him stronger; a leader is someone willing to give his strength to others that they may have the strength to stand on their own."

— Beth Revis

UNLOCKING THE POWER OF YOUR POTENTIAL

Greatness resides inside each of us, but we often fear the changes that will occur in our lives when we unlock it. It's crazy how I can know exactly what I need to do to accomplish a goal but for some reason, I become paralyzed when it's time to execute. I know which steps to take but a part of me is having an out-of-body experience, looking at those steps, and afraid to move forward because I am afraid of the greatness that I know lies within me. I am afraid to unlock that potential and see what the future will hold.

This may sound crazy because a lot of people look at me and think that I am fearless because I am always trying new things, but I am above all else, I am human. I have the same fears, insecurities, and apprehensions as everyone else but one day I came to the realization that I didn't want to leave anything on the table. I do not want to die with a bunch of 'what ifs,' I should haves, or I could haves. I don't want my knowledge or potential to be buried with me. When my day comes, I don't want anyone to mourn for my potential. I want to be celebrated for taking chances, stepping out on faith, and trying. Even in trying and sometimes failing, I have learned so much about my potential from taking a risk and seeing what happens.

I once had an interview and the host asked me about an event that she considered a failure. When she said, "what was it like when xxx failed?" In my mind, I did not consider the event to be a failure, but it did flop, I can admit that. After the event, I took an assessment and recognized what worked, what didn't, and what should have been done differently. I also recognized that that type of event was not right for my brand, but I took that knowledge and was able to consult with others who planned similar types of events. As long as I am learning a lesson, I don't consider any of my projects or experiences to be a failure. Each one teaches me what I can do better next time and serves as an experience in my coaching and consulting toolbox.

Unlocking the Power of Your Potential

Potential is a tricky thing because it is an unknown variable. What we imagine it to be is not always what it ends up being. We see potential in situations and in people that don't always manifest into what we idealized. However, the potential that we see within ourselves is within our control to unleash. Oddly, many of us downplay our potential to match our reality rather than creating a reality that matches our potential.

It is typically out of fear and a lack of self-confidence that we diminish our potential and settle for what is comfortable. When we are honest with ourselves, we can admit the areas of our lives where we have settled and not truly reached for the stars. Whether it was a relationship or job opportunity, we have often sold ourselves short of what we deserve because we masked our fear as humility. I often wonder what sets the uber-successful apart from those who are just getting by day to day. Honestly, they are not always smarter or more resourceful, but they believe in themselves and have no problem reaching for their potential, even when it is beyond their grasp. Of course, there are other factors that also contribute to their success but when measuring attitude, it is their unwavering belief that they will achieve their goals, no matter what.

Have you ever met someone who you considered mediocre, but they achieved extraordinary success? It could be someone in your industry who you know you are more talented than, but they are receiving opportunities that you believe you deserve. The difference between you and them is reach. They aren't afraid to reach for what they want and take the risk of failing. Every time you reach you will not be successful but that doesn't mean you withdraw your hand and retreat. You either continue reaching or you reach in another direction, but you don't stop. Too often we settle because we don't reach far enough. We reach to a level that is comfortable and settle for whatever we can grasp. However, those that achieve extraordinary success are willing to reach past comfort to get to a level that scares most of us.

In the midst of reaching, whether attaining or not, we grow. We learn something new about the process or about ourselves. Those lessons build our skill sets and knowledge base. As our reach extends, our partnerships grow, and we get closer to our purpose and passion. Failing to reach and living within our comfort zone inhibits our growth and creates stagnation in our lives.

When working with clients, I often tell them that they aren't reaching high enough. I dare them to dream their wildest dream for their future and then work to make it a reality. Many successful people start from the bottom and work their way to an extraordinary position because they refuse to settle at ordinary. They push that extra bit to get to the level that some only dream of. You can look at corporate executives, professional athletics, musicians, and almost every other industry to see people who do not necessarily possess more talent or education than anyone else, but they refuse to settle. They are determined to outwork, out hustle, outperform, out practice, and outdo the competition. In the areas of your life where you have not seen the results that you image, can you honestly say that you are out doing the ordinary to reach extraordinary?

I had a client who wasn't seeing success in an area of her business that a competitor, who she considered inferior, was doing much better. We surmised that the competitor was indeed not better, but she was willing to take some risks that my client had talked herself out of. Once my client realized the necessity of taking some risks, she was able to move past her personal comfort zone and into an area of her industry that many strive for. How often have you talked yourself out a goal because of your fear or insecurity?

It is often said that fear is false evidence appearing real, but I can attest that no matter how false that evidence may be, it feels very real. However, we have to learn to embrace the fear and work past it. Whether it's the fear of success, the fear of failure, the fear of taking a risk, the fear of what others will say; we have to be willing to work past it. You cannot pretend that it does not exist because no matter how crazy it may seem to others, it feels very real to you. You have to understand the origin of the fear and do the work to overcome it. Again, I don't believe in faking it until you make it. I am a firm believer in being an adult and doing the hard work to overcome the things that hold you back so that you can move forward. In the midst of faking, the authentic you will manifest in one way or another. It is inevitable. However, when you do the work to deal with the issue, the authentic you will be present to deal with whatever comes up and to grow from it.

Faking is also a mask for our insecurities. It allows us to hide what is really going on and prevents us from growing. Can we be honest and admit that everyone is insecure about something? People are surprised when I tell them that I am insecure. I can admit that I have a fear of not being good enough. I constantly think that I am not enough, that I haven't accomplished enough, and that I am not doing enough. But I don't let those thoughts cripple me. Instead, I use them as motivational tools. I allow them to push me to do more, to be more, and to work harder. With those motivations, I am often able to achieve things that I would have never dreamed of if I had shrunk and given in to the insecurities. I know that the origins of these insecurities are from the expectations of my childhood. Growing up everyone expected me to achieve so making good grades or getting awards was not celebrated. I never knew when I was doing well so I kept working hard waiting for the feeling of accomplishment. Rather than giving in to the thought that no one cares so why bother, I embrace the notion that I can do more, I can be more, I can achieve more, and I keep reaching without setting boundaries for myself. The sky is truly the limit. If I believe it, I can achieve it by reaching and working for it.

Whatever you are afraid of or uncomfortable with about yourself, when you do the work to overcome it, it pushes you past ordinary and into another realm of achieving your potential. You may not be able to clearly define what you believe your potential is but you can probably identify some areas of your life that you need to upgrade. By unlocking the power of your potential, you are automatically upgrading yourself. By taking the brakes off of what you consider impossible and walking in the I'm possible; you will begin to reach further than before.

Imagine the worker who started out as a janitor in the office building but saw people sitting at computers and wearing nice clothes instead of a uniform. The dream of one day becoming one of those people is planted as a seed in their potential. Finding out what they do and researching how to do that job becomes the water in their garden of potential. Taking the steps to prepare for the job is the fertilizer. Obviously, there is no guarantee that they will get a job in that office building but by expanding their potential they have acquired the skills to apply for that same type of job with other companies. This example can be used in many different scenarios.

Dare to dream a life that you are excited about living. Whether it requires a minor change or a major change, step outside of your fear and insecurity to determine what do you need to do to make your dream a reality? Forget about the things that can stop you[1] and begin reaching.

---

[1] This does not apply to specialized industries that require special skills such as becoming a surgeon or professional athlete. Determine what resources you need to achieve the dream and create a plan of action. Make sure you set SMART goals to achieve the dream.

Let's think about your potential...
What do I want to accomplish in my life?

_____

_____

_____

What is stopping me from achieving the goal?

_____

_____

_____

Who told me that I couldn't?

_____

_____

_____

#PowerofP

What is your big idea?

_____

_____

_____

How realistic is the idea?

_____

_____

_____

What can you do to make it attainable?

_____

_____

_____

Unlocking the Power of Your Potential

Who do you need to help you?

_____

_____

_____

What resources do you need?

_____

_____

_____

Other Thoughts:

#PowerofP

I will unlock the power of my POTENTIAL by...

My vision of my potential:

My goal for my potential:
(Is it SMART?)

#PowerofP

Beginning today, I will:

"As you enter positions of trust and power, dream a little before you think."
— Toni Morrison

UNLOCKING THE POWER OF YOUR PRESENTATION

Substance separates the winners from the pretenders. As you've noticed, I have an issue with people who say you have to fake it until you make it.

Prepare and present your best material. I don't always feel the most confident because I know that there are people who do what I do, and they are much better than I am at it. But I don't focus on what someone else is doing. I show up with my best presentation. I make sure that I know my material inside and out, upside and down. In whatever space I am called to show up, I put all of my emotions aside and ensure that I deliver because, at the end of the day, that's what matters most.

It can be easy to get caught up with being impressive, trying to build a following, or even working this gig in anticipation of the next gig but to have longevity in whatever you are doing; substance will always trump style. I have lost count of the number of professionals who have come on the scene and claimed their fifteen seconds of fame but a year or two later they are nowhere to be found. Substance is the secret ingredient of long-term success.

Unlocking the Power of Your Presentation

It doesn't matter if I am presenting to two or three, two hundred, or three thousand; I put the same amount of effort into preparing because I believe everyone deserves the best that I have to offer. I remember being invited to preach at a church because the pastor was away. When I showed up, there were three people in the congregation. I preached the same sermon, possibly better because I was able to personalize it to fit the visual demographic of the members, that I would have preached if the church was packed.

By consistently focusing on being my best, I don't have to try to become something or someone, I can just be. Think about that for a second. Think about the freedom that comes from just being you. Not faking being fabulous. Not trying to be terrific. Not pretending to be perfect. Just being you.

It is a wonderful feeling. Stop faking and start preparing so that you can be!

What goes in will come out. I find that some people have a problem whether speaking in public spaces or networking in small groups because they don't know what to talk about. It is often that simple. The fear and insecurity of presenting comes from a lack of subject matter knowledge.

Luckily, this is something that can be easily overcome. The information that you ingest will be the information that you draw upon for conversation. Needless to say, if the totality of your information consumption is from social media, your conversation will be extremely limited. Even if you are following knowledgeable people, you will only be regurgitating their opinions about subjects.

Once you determine what you are passionate about and what your purpose is, spend time learning more about those things. As you are setting goals for yourself, set the bar high. Aim to become a subject matter expert. Strive to become someone that others are quoting. If you are reading this book, I am assuming that you don't want to settle for average in your life, so I am holding you to a higher standard in every area of your life. You can no longer settle for being like everyone else, doing just enough to get by, coasting through life and blending in. It's time for you to step it up a notch.

What are you reading? You should be reading at least one book per month. Don't like to read? Try audio books to listen while you work out or during your work commute.

What are you watching? Hopefully, your television diet is more than reality television. Turn in to the history channel, the food channel, or watch a documentary. Anything that builds your knowledge base.

What are you eating? I am the last person to advocate for a strict diet because I love cheeseburgers, but I do encourage a balanced diet. If you have a low energy level, it may have something to do with your diet. Make sure you are injecting some vegetables into your meals.

What are you drinking? Too much coffee, tea, or soda can be harmful to your health. Make sure you are drinking enough water to stay hydrated. This also helps to keep your mind sharp.

How are you caring for your mind and body? Are you taking time to reflect on your thoughts so that you can be clear about the direction you want your life to flow? Are you exercising or at least taking regular walks so that you can keep your blood flowing?

What are you listening to? Who are you listening to? The people who you have conversation with are influential to your thought processes because they help to influence how you process information and often your point of view on some subjects, especially those you may find yourself less versed on. It can be easy to rely on those who we deem to be smarter than ourselves to help us understand complex issues. In this case, read the same article from several different sources to distinguish the nuances that one article or writer may have missed.

All of these factors contribute to your presentation. Once you decide the type of person that you want to become, you have to ingest information that will feed that part of yourself. What you feed will grow. If you are not feeding the parts of your life that you want to grow, how can you expect to have anything substantial to contribute to spaces and conversations? When attending conferences or networking events, I read the top articles from several news sources so that I can connect, on some level, with anyone I meet.

People who are faking it don't take the time to actually change their habits. They pretend to make little changes to get by for an event or for an occasion or they make superficial changes. Not doing the hard work of reflecting on what needs to change in your life so that you can become the person you envision will always having you feel insecure and like a fraud because you will know that you did not put in the work to be who you are pretending to be.

Unlocking the power of your presentation is about more than your conversation with others or speaking to a group. It's about presenting yourself, your authentic self, to the world just as you imagine yourself to be. That change may not happen overnight, depending on your goals, but it is something that you can work toward. You may even fall off the wagon. It happens. But the important thing is that you keep your dreams in focus and continue doing the work to achieve them. Don't allow fear and insecurity to cause you to put the mask back on. Remove the mask and work for the life you want. No one is going to give it to you, but you want to unlock the powers within yourself that will make space for it.

So often we place our focus on the physical presence without taking the time to work on the substance that backs up the first impression. Many people say that you don't get a second chance to make a first impression. That's not always true. Sometimes our first impression can be so forgettable that we meet someone, and they have forgotten the first meeting. I don't want that to be you. I want you to be so authentically yourself and comfortable in your own skin that you leave a memorable impression on everyone that you meet.

#PowerofP

Let's think about your presentation…

What do I love to talk about?

_____

_____

_____

What am I reading?

_____

_____

_____

What do I enjoying watching on television?

_____

_____

_____

Unlocking the Power of Your Presentation

Where do I primarily get updates on current events?

_____

_____

_____

How do I ingest the information and formulate my own opinion?

_____

_____

_____

Whose voice do I trust to give me advice?

_____

_____

_____

#PowerofP

How would I rate my energy level?

_____

_____

_____

How would I rate my eating habits?

_____

_____

_____

How would I rate my drinking habits?

_____

_____

_____

How many hours of sleep do I get each night?

_____

_____

_____

How will working on what I internalize effect my presentation going forward?

_____

_____

_____

Other Thoughts:

#PowerofP

I will unlock the power of my PRESENTATION by…

#PowerofP

My vision for my presentation:

My goal for my presentation:
(Is it SMART?)

Beginning today, I will:

> "I wonder if fears ever really go away, or if they just lose their power over us."
> — Veronica Roth

UNLOCKING THE POWER OF PAIN

This is the hardest power for many of us to unlock because pain often feels so senseless, so unnecessary, and most of all, so unwelcome. I have felt this way on many days, but I always remind myself that my pain will not last forever. Whether it is the physical pain of a migraine, the heartbreaking pain of a break-up, or the dulling pain of death; it does not last always. Eventually, the pain subsides, and I move on to the next emotion. However, the pain serves as a reminder that I am alive!

Whatever hurt me, it didn't kill me. When the pain passes, I stand victorious as a survivor. And when the situation returns, when I feel that pain again, I remember that I made it through once and I will make it through again. I remember that even if it's a different type of pain, I will still survive it. My pain helps me to recognize my passion. My pain causes me to pray. My pain influences my purpose. My pain motivates my presence and presentation. My pain causes me to pause to figure out where it is coming from, what is hurting.

In 2004 I was diagnosed with Type 1 Diabetes. Within a matter of weeks, I went from living a carefree life to having to cut carbs, cut out drinking, and injecting myself with insulin several times a day. Some people say that they are sorry for me. For a while, I was sorry for myself. I was in a full pity party. However, it took some serious introspection for me to see the blessing in my diagnosis. Diabetes required me to pause and assess my life. I had to reconsider almost every, once routine decision that I was making in my life. Despite the pain of this diagnosis, I had to choose whether it would stop me from living up to my potential or if I was going to reach for the life that I imagined for myself. I could have easily used it as an excuse to stay in the pause mode, but I chose to allow the pain to motivate me to change. Rather than look down at my situation, I recognized how changing my diet would be beneficial for my health overall. I knew that I couldn't continue drinking like I was, and this was the impetus for my change. My pain gave me an excuse to become more of who I already wanted to be.

The hardest pain that I have had to deal with is the pain of death. I know that I am not alone in this sentiment because we have all lost people who we cared for. The loss of my grandmothers affected me the most. They were the most influential figures in my formative years. I saw them being strong, independent women who raised children, took care of their husbands, maintained a household, and loved God. They pushed me to get an education and to live a life that I could be proud of. Knowing that neither of them are here to see the fruit that has grown from the seeds they planted within me is heartbreaking. I take comfort in replaying the many conversations that I had with them and seeing how their influences have shaped me.

Where does it hurt in your life? Your pain may not be physical or an illness, but it can be a sore spot in your life. What areas are uncomfortable for you? Some of us haven't taken the time to stop and think about where it hurts. We push our pain to the side and continue moving forward. Not dealing with your pain is like not getting the oil changed in your car. The car may continue to run but at some point, the engine will falter. How often have you felt yourself on the brink of a meltdown or break down and you had no idea why? You couldn't quite put your finger on it, but you knew something wasn't right. That's your check engine light coming on and telling you to stop and deal with a pain point in your life.

Whether it is your health, the loss of a relationship, an occurrence from your past, or something said that hurt your feelings; we all experience pain. Society has taught us that pain has to be numbed. Rather than dealing with it, we are taught that we need to suppress it. I challenge that thought and encourage you to figure out what's really wrong and to deal with it.

When we feel pain in our body, we often ignore it until it becomes so severe that we end up going to the doctor's office or find ourselves in the emergency room. Usually, our body has been giving us signs that something was wrong, but we choose to dismiss the symptoms or to self-diagnosis because we think we don't have time to deal with it. Caring for your physical self is perhaps one of the most important things that you can do to contribute to your success. You have to admit, it can be more difficult to take over the world if you are sick. Getting regular check-ups is essential for your wellness and listening to your body. When you are practicing your pause, listen to your body. Listen to each limb and section to see if there are any pain points. Be honest with your physician, ask for treatment options because some issues can be dealt with through a change in diet or exercise, and follow the advice. Don't think that it will go away in time. Your body may get used to it and stop sending you alerts while the problem continues to grow and develop into something more significant.

There is a pain that we have a hard time discussing and that is the pain from mental illness. Unlike a physical pain that allows you to point to a specific part that is ailing, mental illness typically manifests as an unsettling feeling. I am not a mental health expert, but I have suffered from minor bouts of depression. It is hard to get people to understand how your world can go from an array of colors and possibilities to feeling like you are being swallowed by a dark hole and not wanting to get out of bed for days. The hopelessness and inability to function at your optimal level can be difficult to share with others but more importantly, it can be hard to admit within ourselves. But sometimes, you have to say, I am not ok. Dealing with your situation will depend upon the severity of your unrest. For me, it requires taking a hard pause and regrouping. For others, it requires seeking therapy or getting medication. Just as with your physical health, you need to commit to doing whatever it takes to get healthy without regard for the opinions of others.

Dealing with the death of a loved one creates a dull pain that can be inconsolable. People in our lives mean well when they attempt to share words of comfort, but those words rarely have any impact. Allow yourself time to feel the pain. Too often we attempt to be ok to make those around us feel comfortable, but you have no obligation to protect or manage the feelings of others. Day by day the pain lessens but the time is different for every person and is typically dependent on the relationship that you had with the person. The death of my maternal grandmother, who was like a mother to me, still hurts 13 years later. I think about her less than I did ten years ago but the pain is still there. I talk about her and share my grief less, but it is still there. My paternal grandmother departed less than a year from the publication of this book. I didn't go to the funeral because I could not bring myself to see her. There are people in my family who didn't understand or who may have misinterpreted my actions as me not caring but we all grieve in different ways. Allow yourself time to feel whatever feelings you have and to deal with your grief in ways that help you to remain in a healthy headspace.

We often feel pain because of the people in our lives. They can say something that hurts our feelings. They do things that upset us. This is one area where you do have control. As my best friend would say, Use your words. Do not allow yourself to feel powerless in your relationships with others. If something is bothering you, if you are hurt, if you are angry or even disappointed; value yourself enough to express how you are feeling. Don't think that your feelings don't matter or that you are not important. Have the confidence to verbalize what you are feeling. You cannot control how the person responds but you will know that you made your feelings known. Oftentimes, people don't know that have offended us until we tell them. Letting them know gives them a chance to correct their behavior. If they care about the relationship, they will take steps not to continue the behavior. If their behaviors are intentional and they continue, it will be up to you to determine if you want to remain in relationship with the person.

Unlocking the power of your pain helps you to understand what matters to you and who matters to you. Hopefully, you matter enough to take care of your mental and physical health. Those two are no one's responsibility but your own. The pain experienced through our relationships with others help us to see who is important to us. It is impossible to be in relationship with people and not get hurt. It is not because they are bad people but because we are all human and we make mistakes. We sometimes do things without thinking. In the course of our day to day living, we make decisions that impact others. Do not take it personally when some does something that hurts you indirectly.

Direct attacks are in a different category and should be dealt with seriously. However, indirect hurts should be addressed and given an opportunity for correction.

No matter how your pain manifests, do not downplay its effects or put on your mask to make others believe that you are ok. Where does it hurt? What do you need to do for yourself to stop the pain? What has the pain taught you about your priorities?

Healing from our pain also helps us to be better partners. You should not make the current people in your life suffer for the transgressions committed by people from your past. However, when you fail to heal from those past hurts, you carry the memory of those situations into your next relationship. We have to recognize not only what someone else did to cause us pain but also how we contributed to the situation. We even have to recognize instances where we are causing others pain. As we stated earlier, partnerships are a two-way street and we should take care of the people who are in our lives. Just as we don't want them to hurt us directly or indirectly, we should strive to avoid the same.

Let's think about your pain...
Where does it hurt?

_____

_____

_____

How does my pain make me stronger?

_____

_____

_____

Who has caused me pain?

_____

_____

_____

Unlocking the Power of Pain

How do I deal with people who hurt me?

_____

_____

_____

What situations are/were painful to me?

_____

_____

_____

How am I working to overcome that pain?

_____

_____

_____

How has my pain helped me to see what is important to me?

_____

_____

_____

How do I deal with disappointments?

_____

_____

_____

How do I handle break ups?

_____

_____

_____

Unlocking the Power of Pain

How do I handle death?

_____

_____

_____

Who have I hurt?

_____

_____

_____

How can I make up for the pain that I have caused someone?

_____

_____

_____

Other Thoughts:

Unlocking the Power of Pain

I will unlock the power of my PAIN by…

#PowerofP

My vision to deal with my pain:

My goal to deal with my pain:
(Is it SMART?)

Beginning today, I will:

"The measure of a man is what he does with power."

— Plato

UNLOCKING THE POWER OF PERSISTENCE

And I persist.

Have you seen the graphic of the two men in cartoons side by side, each digging to get to their destination, and just as they are about to reach the destination, one turns around and walks away? That has been each of our story at least once, and we may not have even known how close we were to the goal.

I have been self-employed for almost fifteen years. I had to create several streams of revenue to sustain my business – consulting, writing business plans, presenting leadership training for corporations, authoring books, coaching, designing websites – because allowing my business to fail is not an option. Each day when I wake up, I have a goal and whether I reach the goal or not, I spend the day working toward that goal. I may not achieve it that day but some days I hit the gold mine. It's not because that day was so great, but it is because of all of the work that I had put in the days before. If I gave up when it was hard, when I didn't feel like it, when people were uncooperative; I would not be where I am today.

Am I where I want to be? By no means do I feel like I am even close, but I am much further along than I would be if I had stopped trying.

So, I persist.

One of my struggles with persisting is figuring out when I should press and when I should pause. I have found myself in situations where I was unsure if I should continue pressing toward the goal or if I needed to stop and be still. In those moments, my prayer life has helped me to get in tune with God's will for my life. It can be frustrating to not get an immediate answer, but it also strengthens me to know that I have to be deliberate about my decisions and continue to look forward. Even if I am pausing, I am thinking about what is next, creating a plan for the next thing, and waiting for the moment to press.

No matter what happens along this journey, you can not give up on your dreams and goals. Every day you have to commit yourself to getting up and reaching. Each day that you reach will help you to get closer and closer to the sweet spot. If you stop reaching, you will stop getting closer.

Society has fed us another fallacy – that we will one day arrive at this perfect place in life where everything becomes easy. Sadly, many of us live our lives yearning for that day. Each day that is filled with difficulties feels like we are getting further from the happily ever after. I don't believe that happily ever after exists. I believe we wake up every day and we reach for happiness. We do the things that we are passionate about to bring us joy. We live in our purpose to feel fulfilled. We pause to reflect on what is good in life and to hear what our bodies are trying to tell us. We live as our authentic selves so that we can be comfortable in our own skin and our clothes. We surround ourselves with people who help to make us stronger and encourage us to keep reaching. Each day that we are able to do any combination of those things is a good day.

Even on the days when it all goes wrong, we keep reaching. Some days we have the energy and determination to reach further than other days but no matter what, we persist. No matter what it looks like around us, we persist.

Unlocking the Power of Persistence

You can achieve whatever you put your mind to when you commit to unlocking the power of your persistence. It is easy to give up and to settle but reaching for the stars is the hard work. It doesn't happen overnight and that can also be frustrating. We see others living their best lives and we are ready to live ours too. But we don't know how long they were digging to get to that point. Some people look at my business and think that I just popped up on Forbes. They don't know that I have been laying a foundation for close to fifteen years to get to this point. I don't feel the need to argue with them or to explain myself or my success because I am still reaching. I have my goals set much higher.

In the midst of your reaching, find joy in the journey. Take vacations to disconnect and recharge your batteries. Go to bed at night so that you can wake up refreshed and ready to conquer the day. None of this works if you are not taking care of yourself. Your power is within you. You cannot illuminate with some one's light. You cannot use artificial light because it is not going to last.

You must persist through doubt. You must persist through denials. You must persist through disappointment. You must persist through disasters. You must persist every single day.

I am sure there is a part of you that says, this sounds easy, but it is more difficult than I am making it seem. Actually, it isn't. One of the keys to unlocking your power to persist is making up your mind that you will. It takes just as much energy to think of all of the ways that a plan won't work as it takes to develop strategies to make it work. We often place more emphasis on what will go wrong or what is already wrong rather than having a solution-oriented mindset. Before giving up, look backward to see how far you have come and take a look at where you are trying to go. Is it worth turning around and going back now? Or, can you muster the energy to continue going?

Here comes the tricky point, you will reach some situations where you will have to discern whether to persist or to pause. This is an area where many people struggle because you find yourself committed to achieving a goal, but things get difficult, you get tired, and you begin to wonder if you are truly heading in the right direction and doing what you felt lead to do. You wonder if this is the time to persist or pause. This is where the power of prayer is useful. Take some time during your quiet time to think through whether this goal aligns with your passion and purpose. Think through whether you have the necessary partnerships to achieve the goal. During this reflection time, you should be able to discern whether to pause or persist.

It important that you listen to your inner guide and not persist simply because you started. Sometimes we go down a road, like telling people that you are planning to go to Law School, and we don't know how to stop. Once you start studying for the LSAT and begin applying to schools, you realize that you are no longer interested. What do you do? You have told everyone that you are planning to become a lawyer but now the opportunity doesn't interest you. Do you persist in moving forward with something you are no longer interested in? Do you create a new goal that more closely aligns with your passion and purpose? It doesn't matter what you decide as long as you continue pressing forward toward those things that give your life meaning. Of course, most of us crave affirmation, but we should not work toward affirmation because it will satisfy you for a little while, but it will not generate the internal joy that sustains us during difficult times.

Unlocking the power of your persistence will be one of the tools that separates you from others in your industry. For those with a problem-focused mindset, they will find excuses to stop or to continue looking backward. With your solution-oriented mindset, you will remain focused on pressing forward even when you have to take a moment to pause and regroup. Even when you pause, it does not mean that you stop pressing toward the goal. It simply means that you take some time to ensure your vision is in tune with your passion and purpose, that your goals are SMART, and that you have the tools, resources, and partnerships necessary to be successful.

Let's take a look at your persistence...
What are my goals?

_____

_____

_____

How do I handle disappointment?

_____

_____

_____

How do I react to denials?

_____

_____

_____

Unlocking the Power of Persistence

How do I deal with delays?

_____

_____

_____

What have I been working on the longest?

_____

_____

_____

What is stopping me from achieving success?

_____

_____

_____

#PowerofP

How badly do I really want it?

_____

_____

_____

Other Thoughts:

I will unlock the power of my PERSISTENCE by…

My vision of persistence in my life:

My goal for persistence in my life:
(Is it SMART?)

#PowerofP

Beginning today, I will:

> *"What a curious power words have."*
>
> — *Tadeusz Borowski*

UNLOCKING THE POWER OF YOUR PEN

At the time of publication, this is my tenth published book. I say that not to brag but to help you understand how important I believe publishing your work is. Some people write because they think it is going to make them famous, to get more speaking engagements, or they have hopes of becoming a best-selling author.

I have a different motivation. Writing is my legacy. It is how my great great great grandchildren will have insight into my thoughts and lifestyle. It is how they will understand what was happening culturally during my lifetime. When I was researching for a previous book, I had to read some slave narratives to help me understand the context of my work. If those slaves had not penned their stories, not in hopes of fame or fortune but to provide insight; many of us would not have a real understanding of the extent of their struggle. Journaling, blogging, publishing, or any other method of recording your story is not only for you but it is a way of telling your future generations how you got over. We have lost so much of our history because it was never documented. We are now in a position to change that. We can record our stories in a variety of mediums, from a variety of perspectives to aid our future generations with understanding the times that we live in. We can't count on the history books to accurately tell our stories, but we can tell it ourselves.

You do not have to be a great writer to begin writing. Simply writing with a stream of consciousness in a journal is a great way to start if you aren't a writer. Even if you aren't sure of what to write, just start with whatever is on your mind. You can write about your day, your relationship, your dreams, your plans for the future, or you can write creatively and makeup stories. You can write whatever comes to mind. Hopefully, while reading and working through this book you have begun to identify some topics to expound upon and continue writing about.

Writing is a great activity to incorporate in your daily pause. Take some time to center yourself and listen to yourself. From there start writing whatever flows from your mind to your pen.

Unlocking the power of pen can be therapeutic. It can provide you with an opportunity to release information and ideas that may be swimming in your head and help you to organize those thoughts. From hurt feelings to grief to figuring out who you are and what you want in life, your journal is a great place to capture that information. Throughout this book, you have been given writing prompts to help you think more deeply about the material that we have been discussing. Do the work in the areas that you know you need work and use the lessons that you are learning as a tool to help someone else.

If you think you are ready for blogging, there are several online platforms that allow you to post written or video commentary. I caution you to take some time before blogging to identify who your target audience is and what you want to talk about. Once you post information online, you cannot take it back. Even if you delete the blog site or the post, there is no guarantee that the content has not been catalogued somewhere. Don't post anything that you don't want the world to know, no matter what the privacy settings may say. Again, if you are going to share your personal story, ensure it is from a healthy place, a place where someone can learn from your experience. Your online community is not the space to vent your frustrations or to ramble endlessly. In the public sphere your writing should be informational, motivational, inspiring, or building to a call to action.

Have a focus. Consider what the theme of your blog site will be and commit to publishing at least one new article per week. You may also have several themes if you are considering a lifestyle blog. When I started writing, I would share my favorite recipes, interviews with people in my network, relationship advice, and business advice. This allowed me to build a diverse community of followers. Your blog posts should not be more 750 words and should provide the reader with information in a clear, concise, and grammatically correct format. If you are not a great writer, use an editing software to check, double check and triple check your writing for spelling and grammar.

Once you have built an audience, you may be ready to publish a book. I have worked with so many people who jump into publishing a book without having an audience or any experience with writing. How do you know what people want to read from you? How do you know who will buy from you? Friends and family members will account for some of your sales, but you need to build an audience to have someone to interact with your work. Even if you don't sell a million copies, you should build a community around the topic that you are writing about. The ultimate goal with publishing your work is for the longevity but while you are here, give your work some meaning by connecting it with people who are interested in your subject matter.

Even if you don't plan to publish your writing in a blog or in a book, I still suggest journaling. It is not only therapeutic as previously mentioned but it is also a part of the legacy that you can leave for future generations of your family. A family that I am close with found journals that had been written almost 100 years ago by the matriarch of their family. Although they have no plans to publish the words publicly, they have found them to be very useful in getting to know more about the history of their family and to share their family history with future generations. Can you imagine the descendants of your family reading your words 100 years from now? Can you imagine how exciting it would be for them to know what you were thinking and how you were processing all of the social and political events?

Unlocking the power of your pen can unlock some of your deepest emotions as well as create a potential path to profit and serve as a part of your legacy. Remember, you don't have to be a great writer. Spellcheck and grammar programs are your friend. If necessary, hire someone to proofread your work before going public.

Let's take a look at your pen...
How can I find joy in writing?

_____

_____

_____

Am I ready to tell my story?

_____

_____

_____

What other information am I passionate about sharing?

_____

_____

_____

Who would be my target audience?

_____

_____

_____

Do I want to make my writing public or do I prefer to keep it private?

_____

_____

_____

What do I want future generations to know about this amazing life that I am living?

_____

_____

_____

#PowerofP

How can I use the power of my pen to share my message with the world or future generations?

_____

_____

_____

Other Thoughts:

I will unlock the power of my PEN by…

#PowerofP

My vision for using my pen:

My goal for using my pen:
(Is it SMART?)

#PowerofP

Beginning today, I will:

Our Deepest Fear[2]
By Marianne Williamson

Our deepest fear is not that we are inadequate.
Our deepest fear is that we are powerful beyond measure.
It is our light, not our darkness
That most frightens us.

We ask ourselves
Who am I to be brilliant, gorgeous, talented, fabulous?
Actually, who are you *not* to be?
You are a child of God.

Your playing small
Does not serve the world.
There's nothing enlightened about shrinking
So that other people won't feel insecure around you.

We are all meant to shine,
As children do.
We were born to make manifest
The glory of God that is within us.

It's not just in some of us;
It's in everyone.

And as we let our own light shine,
We unconsciously give other people permission to do the same.
As we're liberated from our own fear,
Our presence automatically liberates others.

---

[2] Williamson, M. (1996) **A Return to Love: Reflections on the Principles of "A Course in Miracles",** New York, NY: HarperOne

I hope you have found the power within you that will allow you to accomplish any goal that you set your mind to. I hope that there is nothing in your past, present, or future that you will allow to impede whatever you hope to achieve. Whether you accomplish the task or fall woefully short, learn the lesson from the experience so that you can use it as a building block in your toolbox.

Don't ever play small and pretend that you are not exactly who you were created to be. Share your gifts of passion and purpose with the world so that the gifts of others will be returned to you.

Don't ever shrink to fit a situation or to make others feel bigger or better about themselves. Show up everywhere you go as your best and most authentic self. You don't have to fake it when you are comfortable in your own skin

It took me a long time to learn the lessons that I have shared with you in this book and because of that, I am fiercely protective of the person that I have worked hard to become. I hope you will be also and that you will not allow anyone to stand in the way of you walking in the life that you have designed.

Go forth and live your best life!

La'Kesha

P.S.
Don't forget to tag me on social media using #PowerofP to share some of the strategies that you have developed to unlock the best parts of yourself. I would love to hear from you.

"Your greatest power is in your ability to deal with and overcome whatever life throws at you. Don't worry about it getting easier, focus on becoming better because of it!"

— LaKesha Womack

ABOUT THE AUTHOR – LAKESHA WOMACK

LaKesha Womack is the Owner and Lead Consultant with Womack Consulting Group. The firm provides Business Development, Brand Management, Leadership Training, Strategic Planning, and Political Consulting to clients across the globe through consultations with professionals, not for profit organizations, churches, colleges/universities, and businesses of all sizes. She has served as a business development presenter for numerous Chambers of Commerce and professional groups. She specializes in working newly formed teams, fractured teams, and boards of directors to teach leadership and professional development strategies to enhance communication, build brand recognition, and improve meeting effectiveness.

LaKesha has a bachelor's degree from Vanderbilt University, is a graduate of the Women's Campaign School at Yale University, and is pursuing a master's degree from Chicago Theological Seminary. She is a member of the Forbes' Coaches Council as a thought leader on leadership topics and contributes to Forbes.com with more than forty business tips provided on their Expert Panel forum. LaKesha is the published author of ten books and has been featured in numerous publications and interviews providing financial literacy tips, business advice, and community engagement strategies.

LaKesha is also the founder of LaKesha's Leadership Circle, a membership platformed designed to empower leaders with the tools and resources to achieve their goals. She is active within her community as a Minister in the African Methodist Episcopal Zion Church and as a member of the National Coalition of 100 Black Women – Queen City Mecklenburg County Chapter.

For media inquiries or to book LaKesha for an event, visit BookLaKesha.com.

Made in the USA
Columbia, SC
24 February 2024